The American Journalists

THE DEMOCRATIC JUDGE; OR
THE EQUAL LIBERTY OF THE PRESS

William Cobbett

ARNO
&
The New York Times

Collection Created and Selected
by Charles Gregg of Gregg Press

Reprint edition 1970 by Arno Press Inc.

LC# 70-125686
ISBN 0-405-01663-8

The American Journalists
ISBN for complete set: 0-405-01650-6

Reprinted from a copy in
The State Historical Society of Wisconsin Library

Manufactured in the United States of America

THE

DEMOCRATIC JUDGE:

OR THE

EQUAL LIBERTY of the PRESS,

AS

Exhibited, Explained, and Expoſed,

In the Prosecution of

WILLIAM COBBETT,

For a pretended Libel againſt

The King of Spain and his Embaſſador,

BEFORE

THOMAS M'KEAN,

Chief Justice of the State of Pennsylvania.

By PETER PORCUPINE.

PHILADELPHIA:

PUBLISHED BY WILLIAM COBBETT, OPPOSITE CHRIST-CHURCH

March, 1798.

Advertisement.

I KNOW it has been thought, that *I was afraid* to publish an account of the prosecution carried on against me by the State Government of Pennsylvania, at the instance of the Spanish Minister. I can readily excuse people for entertaining this opinion, because the American press is become the most tame, the most humbled, the most abject upon the face of the earth; and because I count it no dishonour not to be thought a match for the dangers to which I am exposed. The opinion will, however, be found to be eroneous. I have, in the following sheets, exhibited this unparalleled proceeding to the world in its true colours; and I take this opportunity of declaring my fixed determination to persevere in rendering equally notorious, every fact, of which such like proceedings shall put me in possession.—My daily occupations leave me but little time for undertakings of this sort; but my just resentment, though slow in its operation, shall not be less sure in its effects.

WILLIAM COBBETT.

Philadelphia, March 9th, 1798.

INTRODUCTION.

JUDGE M'KEAN, the Chief Justice of Pennsylvania, in his charge to the Grand Jury (of which the reader will see enough by-and-by), observed, that " *the liberty of the press* was a " phrase much used, but little understood." This, in a *public servant*, as all the democratic officers call themselves, is making pretty free with the understanding of the sovereign people, and of a people too whom the Congress have declared *free* and *enlightened*, and would have declared the "*free-est* and most *enlightened in the world*," had it not been for their desire " to avoid all *cause* " *of offence*" towards the *free* and *enlightened* French.*

The Judge was certainly wrong. No people understand what the liberty of the press means better than the Americans do. No one knows so well how to appreciate the value of a thing, as he who has long enjoyed, and then lost it.

---

* See *Censor* for December, 1796, for a full account of this humiliating business.

Had the Judge called the liberty of the prefs a thing much talked about, much boafted of, and *very little enjoyed*, I would moft readily have fubfcribed to his affertion; for, of all the countries under the Sun, where *unlicenfed* preffes are tolerated, I am bold to declare, and the contents of this pamphlet will eftablifh the truth of my declaration, that none ever enjoyed lefs *real* liberty of the prefs than America has for fome years paft.

I do not fay, that this liberty has been abridged by any pofitive law; on the contrary, I know well, that feveral of the State Conftitutions hold out a fomething (not very intelligible to be fure) that would feem to extend the liberty of printing beyond the limits prefcribed by the Englifh law. Nor do I pretend, that this dangerous abridgment of American freedom is to be attributed to the change, which the revolution has produced in the name and nature of the government. I will not, for a moment, be faid to infinuate, that the prefs is become not free, merely becaufe the government is become *republican*. No; I think, the people, when they adopted this form of government, expected, as they certainly *were led to expect*, an extention of this, and every other important branch of their liberties. What I contend for, is, that, fome how or other, this liberty has been abridged; the exercife of it, either by popular prejudice, by the influence of party, the fear of mobifh violence, or of governmental tyranny, has been, and yet is, moft fhamefully and difgracefully *restrained*.

To

To enter into the caufes, which have produced this fatal effect, would be to revive the remembrance of what I wifh may ever remain buried in oblivion. I will therefore content myfelf with *proving the fact*; and to do this to the fatisfaction of every candid mind, I need go no farther back than my own times.

When I firft came to Philadelphia, I was charmed with the literary liberty, which its inhabitants feemed to enjoy. I faw pamphlets in every window, and news-papers in every hand. I was, indeed rather furprifed to find, that thofe pamphlets, and thefe news-papers were, fomething like *a certain Judge* that I had heard of, *all on one side:* but, faid I to myfelf, this muft be the fault of the authors and editors; and it leaves, the more room for fuch as have a mind to write on the other fide. With this agreeable but delufive notion in my brain, I fat down contented under the calamity of reading daily, in common with my poor fellow citizens, about eighteen or twenty long columns of the vileft and moft infipid trafh that ever was ftamped upon paper.

Long did I hope, and expect, to fee fomething like a manly and effectual oppofition to this flood of falshood and partiality; but I hoped and expected in vain. At laft, it was *my* fate to enter the field. I had long felt a becoming indignation at the atrocious flander that was continually vomitted forth againft Great Britain; and the malignancy of Prieftley and his addreffers at New-York brought it into action.

The

The OBSERVATIONS on the emigration of this reftlefs and ambitious demagogue contain, as I have elfewhere remarked, " not one untruth, " one anarchical, indecent, immoral, or irreligi- " ous expreffion"; yet, when I came to offer it for the prefs, the bookfeller was afraid it was not *popular enough*. He was far, as he faid, from difapproving of the work ; but it was *too much in favour of Great Britain*, and on this account he thought it would endanger his *windows*, if not his *person*.

This mans fears feemed to me perfectly abfurd. The pamphlet faid not a word in praife of Great Britain, generally. Indeed, policy had led me to fpeak rather harfhly of that nation in one paffage or two ; and fo evident was this, that the *Britifh Critics*, though they pay the author compliments far beyond his merit, cannot forbear to lament, they fay, that fo enlightened a mind fhould ftill harbour *a rancour so implacable*. Thefe people, though certainly not lefs penetrating than GOOSY TOM in the common affairs of literature, would have laughed at the idea of broken windows and bafted carcaffes.

However, notwithftanding the ridicule, which this remark of the BRITISH CRITICS is calculated to throw on the apprehenfions of my bookfeller, now the *worthy partner* of LLOYD, fubfequent events have proved, that thofe apprehenfions were not entirely groundlefs : for, although he did publifh feveral fucceeding pamphlets from the fame pen, without incurring a penalty of any kind, yet no fooner was the *real author* known, than he began to fee, and to feel too,

too, that BRADFORD underſtood the *American liberty of the press* far better than he did.

During the publication of the reſt of the pamphlets that iſſued from BRADFORD'S, I had often to contend with his ſcruples and his fears. In particular, I remember, that my calling the French miniſter ADET, no *Chriſtian*, was very hard to be ſurmounted. The French had openly and moſt blaſphemously *aboliſhed the Chriſtian religion*; and the Convention, who had ſent out this embaſſador, had even formally *denied the being of a God*; yet, ſo high was this bookſeller's notions of the *liberty of the press*, that he was afraid to publiſh a ſentence, in which the French miniſter was ſaid *not to be a Chriſtian*! If as much had been ſaid of the Engliſh miniſter, though falſe, he would, I am pretty confident have had no ſcruples at all.

It was no ſooner diſcovered that I was PETER PORCUPINE, and that I had taken the excellent houſe and ſhop, that I now occupy, in order to carry on the printing and bookſelling buſineſs, than the French faction began to muſter their forces and put themſelves in battle array. Several infamous publications appeared in BACHE's paper, declaring me to be a *deſerter*, a *felon*, a *thief* who had fled from the *gallows*, &c. &c.

Strong in my innocence I ſteadily purſued my courſe, and, thank God, my ſteadineſs was attended with ſucceſs. Stung at the contempt with which I treated theſe abominable attempts on my character, another mode of injuring me
was

was fallen upon. A *threatning letter* was conveyed under the door of my landlord, the base object of which the letter itself will best explain. It is a performance that should ever find a place in a work that treats of the " *unrestrained liberty* " *of the press.*" Here it is.

" To Mr. *John Oldden, Merchant,*

" *Chesnut Street.*

" Sir,

" A certain William Cobbett, alias
" Peter Porcupine, I am informed is your te-
" nant. This daring scoundrel, not satisfied
" with having repeatedly traduced the people
" of this country, vilified the most eminent and
" patriotic characters among us *and grossly abus-*
" *ed our allies the French,* in his detestable pro-
" ductions, has now the *astonishing effrontry* to
" expose those very publications at his win-
" dow for sale, as well as certain prints indica-
" tive of the *prowess of our enemies the British*
" *and the disgrace of the French.* Calculating
" largely upon the moderation or rather pusilla-
" nimity of our citizens, this puppy supposes he
" may even insult us with impunity. But he
" will e'er long find himself dreadfully mistaken.
" 'Tho' his miserable publications have not been
" hitherto considered worthy of notice, the late
" manifestation of his impudence and enmity to
" this country will not be passed over. With a
" view therefore of preventing your feeling *the*
" *blow* designed for him, I now address you.
" When the time of retribution arrives, it may
" not be convenient to discriminate between the
" innocent and the guilty. Your property there-
" fore

" fore may fuffer. For depend upon it brick walls will not fkreen the rafcal from punifh- ment *when once the business is undertaken.* As a friend therefore I advife you to fave your property by either compelling Mr. Porcupine to *leave your house* or at all events oblige him *to cease exposi g his obominable productions* or any of his *courtly prints* at his window for fale. In this way only you may avoid danger to your houfe and perhaps fave the rotten car- cafs of your tenant for the prefent."

"A HINT."
" July, 16th 179C."

It will be remembered, that I inftantly pub-lifhed this letter, accompanied with comments, in which I fet the authors (for they were many) at defiance; but I did not mention then a cir-cumftance that it is proper I fhould mention now. There was, on the morning in which I received the letter, one of the *judges* in my fhop. I fhow-ed it him, and apprized him of my intention of publifhing it in the manner I afterwards did; but he advifed me againft it, for *fear* of *the con-sequences.* This proves his opinion with refpect to the *protection* the liberty of the prefs would receive in Philadelphia.

No violence, however, did fucceed. But the election for members of Congrefs was approach-ing; and, as the *free* men would then be affem-bled, it was feared by my friends; indeed, it was generally underftood, and publickly talked of, that, on the election night, *my house was to be gutted.* And, left the *sans of liberty* fhould
be

be uninformed of the bufinefs, and confequently unprepared for it, the fame wretch BACHE (the Grandfon and pupil of Old Franklin) reminded them of it by an inflammatory publication figned AN AMERICAN, which, after a feries of the moft atrocious falfhoods, concludes thus:
—" while I am a friend to the *unlimited* free-
" dom of the prefs, when exercifed by *an Ame-*
" *rican*, I am an implacable foe to its proftituti-
" on to a *foreigner*, and would at any time affift
" in hunting out of fociety, any meddling fo-
" reigner, who fhould dare to interfere in our
" politics. I hope the *apathy* of our brethren
" of Philadelpnia will no longer be indulged,
" and that an *exemplary vengeance* will foon
" burft upon the head of fuch a prefumptuous
" fellow.—*Juftice, honour, national gratitude,* all
" call for it.—May it *no longer be delayed.*

" *An American.*"

The American who can read this without blufhing is an object of contempt, of fcorn ; a neutralized animal that has no idea of national honour, and that would fell his country, were it in his power, for a fingle Louis d'or. Yet fuch there are, and in abundance too.

A publication like his, the direct and avowed object of which was, to inftigate the *free* men to devaftation and *murder,* fhould, one would think, have been noticed by the magiftrates, particularly under the eye of a *Chief Juftice,* whom we fhall by-and-by fee fo zealous and fo watchful. But, no. It attracted the attention of no one, or at leaft no one took any meafures to prevent the intended affault. My houfe and my family might have been burnt to afhes ; we might all have been dragged into the ftreet and murdered, and, I fincerely believe, not fo much as a conftable would have held up his ftaff to arreſt the aſſaſſins We were, however, prepared for their reception. We fhould not have fallen unrevenged. Some of their fouls would have taken their departure from my door-way on their journey to hell.

It is here that I ought, and that I do with pleafure, acknowledge the generofity of feveral gentlemen of the city (many of whom I never faw), who I was afterwards affured, had formed the refolution to fummon the magiftrates, and to come to my aid in perfon. One gentleman in particular, whom I did not then know even by name, went in difguife among the groups of *free* men to endeavour to find out their intention. I wifh I *durst* name him now ; but my *gratitude* to him forbids me to do it. When *liberty* comes to this pitch, I think it ought to affume fome other name.

But, what was the moft fhameful, and what is moft directly to the point before us, was, this audacious, this cut-throat attack on the liberty of the prefs, was fuffered to pafs unnoticed, not only by all the other preffes in this city, but by all the preffes in the continent. There are, perhaps, two or three hundred news-papers publifhed in the United States, and not one of them have ever whifpered a word in condemnation of it, from that day to this.

If, however, it was proper to deſtroy me; if "*Juſtice, honour*, and *national gratitude*" demanded my blood for exerciſing the liberty of the preſs, that ſame "*Juſtice, honour* and *national gratitude*" did, it ſeems, require my enemies to exerciſe that liberty in *perfect safety*. No leſs than ſeven pamphlets were, in this city, publiſhed againſt me in the ſpace of ten days. It is a pity they cannot now be found above ground. Had they lived, they would have been a laſting honour to the country that gave them birth, and particularly to the *equal* laws and *impartial judiciary* that tolerated them. They were, all together, a compoſition of brutality, ſlander, and villainy of every ſort and deſcription, that would have diſgraced hell itſelf. The anonymous ſcoundrels who wrote them vied with each other in baſeneſs and atrocity; and one of them, who ſeemed reſolved to have the pre-eminence in infamy, and for whom everlaſting damnation is too mild a puniſhment, inſinuated *that my wife was a whore!*—And all this, only becauſe I had written with ſucceſs againſt a nefarious French faction. This is *American liberty of the press!*

Were I to ſet about recounting all the inſtances of perſecution I have experienced; all the menaces I have received; all the vexations through the channel of the poſt-office, &c. &c. I could fill fifty volumes like this. The written threats, which I have now by me, to aſſaſſinate or poiſon me, or fire my houſe, amount to ſome hundreds. Nor is this ſpecies of baſeneſs confined to this city or this ſtate. There is hardly a poſt mark of an American town, which I cannot, and which *I will not*, ſhow ſtamped on ſome
infamous

infamous production, intended, in fome way or other, to reftrain the liberty of my prefs.

I fhall wind up this feries of injuries, of bafe machinations and brutal autrage, that have been attempted againft me, with an anecdote, which cannot fail to give the reader a high opinion of the decency, candour and juftice to be met with in Pennfylvania.—A great beef-headed purblind creature, that calls itfelf a young lawyer, and whofe pleading bears an infinite refemblance to the bleating of an overgrown calf, obferved to * * * * * juft before the court fat, that it was quite wrong to honour me with a *legal* punifhment; and that, if I had ceufured him, as I had done fome other of the *patriots*, he would have clapped a piftol to my *breast* and blowed my *brains* out!—There now, leaving the *bull* afide, is a noble fentiment for you! What fort of juftice has a man to expect, where fuch language can, *in such company*, be held with impunity?—However, I will never fly to the law to fhelter me from the vengence of this bellowing animal, who, inftead of ftanding erect before the bench, ought to be placed on all fours before a rack and manger I will never fly to the law, or to any thing elfe, to fhelter me from the foft horns of this half-grown, blinking, bloated cornuto.

I fhould now enter into a recital of the perfecutions, of various forts, which other printers, not devoted to the French, have experienced; but this would lead me too far. I cannot, however, omit noticing one remarkable inftance of *patriotic liberality* and *justice.*

" *Richmond,*

" *Richmond, Virginia, April* 4, 1794."

" About two weeks ago, a piece was publifhed
" in the Virginia Gazette, requefting all true re-
" publicans *to wear the national cockade*, in ho-
" *our of France*, which, it feems, was not well re-
" ceived by the Ariftocrats. The next day ano-
" ther piece came out, in another of your pa-
" pers, figned, " *A foe to diftinctions.*" ridiculing
" the meafure, comparing thofe citizens who
" adopted it to fools and madmen, which fo irri-
" tated the *republican party*, that fome of them
" waited on the printer, and demanded the au-
" thor. He told them, he did not know who he
" was, and would go before a magiftrate and
" *take his oath of it.* I affure you he was *greatly*
" *alarmed* on the occafion, and I think has loft
" much of his intereft by it.—They were not fa-
" tisfied with this ; but, in the evening erected a
" *gallows*, fixed it on a waggon carriage, hung
" the poor fellow up in effigy, and paraded
" through the ftreets beating the *rogue's* march.
" At laft they ftopped before the poft-office
" door, and burnt him with repeated fhouts and
" huzzas.—I am confident, if they could have
" found the author, he would have fuffered the
" *same fate* as the effigy ; at leaft they would
" have complimented him with a fuit of *Ameri-*
" *can* manufacture, extracted from the *lofty pine*,
" and the filling taken from a *goose*.—You fee
" what the Virginians *dare* do—what they do to
" enemies of *liberty*—and I fincerely hope all
" who are inimical to the caufe of America, *or*
" *France*, may meet a fimilar reward."

This

This extract is taken from BACHE's paper, No. 1044; and the circumstances of the bafe tranfaction that it recounts were pretty exactly as it defcribes them. This printer was exhibited as a *rogue* that merited to be *hung* and *burnt*; and his author if found, would have actually fuffered this ignominious fate: and all this for writing and publifhing—what?—A fenfible effay, advifing the people not to make themfelves appear like fools and madmen, by adopting the fantaftical fopperies, or rather by ranging themfelves under the colours, of a *foreign nation!*—Will any one pretend to fay, that, in a country where fuch unjuft, tyrannical, and inhuman proceedings could take place, and pafs unpunifhed and unnoticed by the civil power; will any one have the effrontery to fay, that, in fuch a country, there is any thing worthy of being called, *the liberty of the press?*—But, no more. It is mere mockery to talk of it.

Now, in anfwer to all this, fome precious villain, deep leaned in the jargon of the *Rights of Man*; or fome temporizing drivler from the canting fchool of *modern republicanism*: fome infamous BACHE or trimming NOAH WEBSTER, will tell me that nothing which I have here advanced, tends to prove the prefs to be in thraldom. They will fay, that fo long as it remains unfhackled by *the law!* fo long as *the law* does not invade its liberty, it is *free*.—No; it is not fo. The law is made to *protect* the weak and the injured, as well as to punifh the guilty. The law which declares, that a man fhall have fuch or fuch a right, guarantees to him the *enjoyment* of that right: therefore, the law which fays,

that

that " *the printing presses shall be free,*" pledges the faith and honour of the nation to *protect them in the exercise of their freedom*; and to fail in yielding them this protection, is as much a breach of the national faith as is an actual invafion of this freedom by the law; for, where is the difference to the printer, whether the law itfelf reftrain his prefs, or fuffer it to be reftrained? I think I hate *a tyrant* (and I think *I have reason*) as much as moft men do! but I would much rather a tyrant fhould order my rights to be furpreffed, than have them rifled from me by his tools, a brutal and ferocious mob

For want of this fo neceffary protection it is, that the infernal French faction have, aided by certain men in power in moft of the State Governments, got the *real* liberty of the prefs into their poffeffion, to the almoft general exclufion of their opponents. For want of this protection it is, that the friends of the Federal Government have been abafhed, humbled, filenced, and, in many inftances, induced to *change sides*: and, it is for want of this protection, that we at this moment fee fuch numbers of infipid, tame and trimming papers, which, under the cowardly guife of *impartiality*, are a difgrace to literature, a difhonour to the country, a clog to the government, and a curfe to the people.

I have now, I think, and in pretty plain language too, proved, that, fome way or other, the liberty of the American prefs has been moft fcandaloufly attacked and reftrained, notwithftanding the *law* declares, *it shall be perfectly free.* What the law itfelf, and thofe who adminifter

nifter that law, are capable of performing in
this way, under the *free* and *equal* and *lenient*
and *hnmane* government of poor Pennfylvania,
it is the object of the following pamphlet to expofe to a deceived and infatuated world.

AMERICAN

AMERICAN

LIBERTY *of the* PRESS,

&c. &c.

W HEN I undertook the publishing of a daily paper, it was with the intention of annihilating, if possible, the intriguing, wicked, and indefatigable faction, which the French had formed in this country. I was fully aware of the arduousness of the task, and of the inconvenience and danger to which it would expose both me and mine. I was prepared to meet the rancorous vengence of enemies in the hour of their triumph, and the coolness of friends in the hour of my peril. in short, to acquire riches seemed to me quite uncertain, and to be stripped of every farthing of my property seemed extremely probable ; but let what would happen, I was resolved to pursue the contemplated object, as long as there remained the most distant probability of success.

Among

Among the dangers, which prefented themfelves to me, thofe to be apprehended from the feverity of the law appeared the moft formidable; more efpecially as I happened to be fituated *in the State of Pennsylvania*, where the government, generally fpeaking, was in the hands of thofe, who had (and fometimes with great indecency) manifefted an uniform partiallity for the fans-culotte French, and as unifom an oppofition to the minifters and meafures of the Federal Government. Thefe perfons I knew I had offended by the promulgation of difagreeable truths; and, therefore, it was natural, that I fhould feek for fome ftandard as a fafe rule for my conduct with refpect to *the liberty of my press*.

To fet about the ftudy of the law of *libels*, to wade through fifty volumes of myfterious tautology, was what I had neither time nor patience to do. The Englifh prefs was faid to be *enslaved*; but, when I came to confult the practice of this enflaved prefs, I found it ftill to be far *too free* for me to attempt to follow its example. Finally, it appeared to me to be the fafeft way, to form to myfelf fome rule founded on the liberty exercifed by the *American press*. I concluded, that I might, without danger, go as great lengths in attacking the enemies of the country as others went in attacking its friends: that as much zeal might be fhown in defending the General Government and adminiftration as in accufing and traducing them: and that as great warmth would be admiffible in the caufe of virtue, order, and religion, as had long been tolerated in the wicked caufe of villainy, infurrection,

infurrection, and blafphemy. What ever rancour might be harboured againft me in the breafts of particular perfons, I depended on *shame* to reftrain the arm of power : I thought no officer or officers of ftate, would, in this country, dare to deal towards an honeft man with a rigour which had never been experienced by the vileft of mifcreants. Alas! "all "this I thought, and all I thought was wrong;" as the following fheets will moft clearly evince.

Before I enter on the account of the groundlefs profecution which this Pennfylvania ftate government has compelled me to fuftain, it is neceffary to notice fome fteps that were taken by my enemies previoufly thereto.

Some time in the month of Auguft laft, the Spanifh Minifter Don Carlos Martinez de'Yrujo, applied to the Federal Government to profecute me for certain matters publifhed in my Gazette, againft himfelf and that poor unfortunate and humbled mortal, Charles the fourth, King of Spain. The government confented, and I was accordingly bound over, before the Honourble Judge Peters, to appear in the Federal diftrict court, which will meet next April.

Of this preparatory ftep to *a fair and impartial* trial the Don was informed. But, it would feem, the information was far from being fatisfactory to him ; for, he delivered in a memorial to the Federal Government, requefting (for what reafon I leave the reader to determine) that the trial might come on before the Supreme Court of Pennfylvania, of which court *M'Kean is Chief Juftice.*

Thus

24

Thus foiled in the grand object, a new scrutiny was, without much regard to decency, set on foot; new pretended libels were hunted out; and, an application to prosecute me was made to the government of Pennsylvania. It is hardly necessary to say that consent was speedily obtained. A bill of indictment was prepared by the attorney Genera lof the state, and a warrant, of which the following is a copy was issued to sieze me.

Pennsylvania ss.

The Commonwealth of Pennsylvania to the Sheriff of the County of Philadelphia, to the Constables of the City of Philadelphia, and to all other OUR Ministers and Officers within OUR said City and County, Greeting.

For as much as the Chief Justice of OUR Supreme Court is given to understand by the information, testimony, and complaint of credible persons, that WILLIAM COBBETT of the City of Philadelphia, printer, is the printer and publisher of certain infamous and wicked libels against His Chatholic Majesty the King of Spain, the Chevalier Charles Martinez de Yrujo envoy extraordinary and minister plenipotentiary of His said Catholic Majesty to the United States of America, and of the Spanish nation, contained in public journals, or news-papers called PORCUPINE'S GAZETTE, numbers 114, 115, 121, 127, 156, 160, 163 and 180, in the said City of Philadelphia, tending to defame the said, King, envoy and minister, and the subjects of the said King, to *alienate their* AFFECTIONS AND REGARD *from the government and citizens of the United States of America* and of US, to excite them to hatred, hostilities and war against the said United States.

Therefore

Therefore WE command you, and every of you, that some, or one of you attach the aforesaid WILLIAM COBBETT, so that you have him as soon as he can be taken before OUR said Chief Justice, to answer US of the premises, and be further dealt withal according to law:— And have you then there this precept. Witness the Honourable Thomas M'Kean, Doctor of Laws, Chief Justice of OUR Supreme Court, at Philadelphia, the Eighteenth day of November in the Twenty second year of the *Indepence* of the United States of America, and in the year of our Lord one thousand seven hundred and ninety seven.

THOMAS M'KEAN.

True Copy.

Jos. Thomas.
Nov. 18, 1797.

If I did not well know, that all instruments of this kind, coming from under the hand and seal of a *Judge*, are, by privilege immemorial, exempted from the lash of criticism, I should most certainly be tempted to try my hand on the warrant.—For instance : the Commonwealth is called us, and this may be proper enough, as the Commonwealth, in the modern stile, means the *citizens thereof*. But, what shall we make of the passage, where it is said, that I endeavoured to alienate the affections of the Spaniards from the citizens of the United States *and of* us ; that is, from the citizens of the United States, *and from the citizens of* us ; and this last sentence means, *from the citizens of the citizens of the Commonwealth* ! In the name of mercy what is all this ! Is the form intended to convey a notion, that the citizens of Pennsylvania have *other citizens* under their controul and government; or that the citizens of the Commonwealth are

their

their own citizens, and that WE govern US?— A projector fome few years ago received a *prize medal* from the philofophical fociety of Philadelphia, for having invented an *American language.* I wonder if this warrant be a fpecimen of it?

But, let *us* return to more folid matter.

The trifling circumftances attending an arreft and giving bail are fcarcely worth relating; but, fometimes, trifling circumftances ferve to convey a more correct idea of the character of the parties concerned in a tranfaction, and to guide the reader to a more juft appreciation of their motives, than the longeft and moft laboured general account of their conduct.

The Sheriff (whofe civility and candour I have every reafon to applaud) came to my houfe, for *the first time,* at twelve o'clock; and he was ordered to have me before the Judge *at half past one.* Thank God, I am not verfed in arrefts; but, I believe, this is the firft time, that ever a man, profecuted for a libel, was pinned down to the fhort fpace of *an hour and a half* to prepare for going out and to procure himfelf bail. The Englifh reader (for this pamphlet fhall be read in England) will obferve, that this government of Pennfylvania, is that which is everlaftingly boafting of the *mildness* and *humanity* of its laws.

I was not fo deftitute of friends as, perhaps, the Judge expected I was. Bail was procured, and we were before him at the appointed time.

He

He afked us to fit down. I feated myfelf on one fide of the fire, and he on the other. After he had talked on for fome time to very little purpofe (at leaft as to the effect his talk produced on me), he fhewed me certain newfpapers, and afked me if *I had printed and published them.* To this I replied, *that the law did not require me to answer any questions in that stage of the business, and that, therefore, I should not do it.* At this reply, though a very prudent and a very proper one, " he waxed exceeding wroth." He inftantly ordered me to get off my chair and ftand up before him, though he himfelf had invited me to fit down. This fpecies of refentment, fo becoming in a *Judge,* excited in my mind no other fentiments than that which I dare fay it has already excited in the mind of the reader.

The next document, which follows in due courfe, is THE BILL OF INDICTMENT; the IGNORAMUS Bill of Indictment.—Go over it with attention, I befeech thee, reader; or elfe, take my word for it, you will be juft as wife when you have done, as you are now. You muft have your eyes well about you; keep a fharp look out for parenthefifes and quotations; and, above all you muft *hold your breath to the bottom of a paragraph*; if you can't do this, you will no more underftand it than you would the croaking of a frog or the cakling of a goofe.— Therefore, again I fay, attention!

OYER

OYER AND TERMINER; November Seſſions, 1797.
Philadelphia County ſſ.

The grand Inqueſt of the Commonwealth of Pennſylvania, upon their oaths and affirmations reſpectively, DO PRESENT: That WILLIAM COBBETT, late of the City of Philadelphia, in the County of Philadelphia, Yeoman, being a perſon of a wicked and turbulent diſpoſition, and maliciouſly deſigning and intending, to vilify and defame the perſon, character, and government, of His Chatholic Majeſty, Charles the fourth, King of Spain, and to diſturb and deſtroy the peace and amity and concord, *now happily ſubſiſting* between the ſame and the United States of America; and alſo, to vilify and defame the perſon and character of Don Carlos Martinez de Yrujo, the miniſter plenipotentiary and envoy extraordinary from His Catholic Majeſty, the ſaid King of Spain, to the United States, ON the ſeventeenth day of July, in the year of our Lord one thouſand ſeven hundred and ninety ſeven, at the City of Philadelphia, in the County aforeſaid, wickedly and maliciouſly did print and publiſh, and cauſe to be printed and publiſhed, a certain *ſcandalous, falſe*, and *malicious* libel, of and concerning His Catholic Majeſty the ſaid King of Spain, and of and concerning the ſaid Don Carlos Martinez de Yrujo, the ſaid miniſter plenipotentiary and envoy extraordinary from His ſaid Majeſty to the United States, in a certain news-paper called PORCUPINE'S GAZETTE, which ſaid newspaper was then and there printed and publiſhed by the ſaid WILLIAM COBBETT, and in the form of obſervations, ſigned by *an old ſoldier*, and directed and addreſſed for PORCUPINE'S GAZETTE; in which ſaid libel are contained; among other *things* and *expreſſions*, divers of falſe, feigned, ſcandalous, and malicious matters, according to the *tenor* following, to wit:—" *Ever ſince Spain has been governed by princes of the Bour-*
" *bon family, the Spaniſh name has been diſgraced in peace and in war;*
" *every important meaſure has been directed by the crooked politics of*
" *France—This connection, like the obſcene harpers of old, contaminates*
" *whatever it touches. But never has this been ſo conſpicuous as in the*
" *preſent reign, and more eſpecially at the preſent period*   The degenerate
" *prince that now ſways the Spaniſh ſceptre* [thereby meaning His Catholic Majeſty, the ſaid King of Spain] *whom the French* [the French Republic meaning] *have kept on the throne merely as a trophy of their power,*
" *or as the butt of their inſolence, ſeems deſtitute not only of the dignity of a*
" *king, but of the common virtues of a man; not content with allying him-*
" *ſelf to the murderers of a benevolent Prince who was the flower of his fa-*
" *mily, he* [His Catholic Majeſty the ſaid king of Spain meaning] *has*
" *become the ſupple tool of all their* [the ſaid French Republic meaning]
" *moſt nefarious politics.   As the Sovereign* [His Catholic Majeſty the ſaid King of Spain meaning] *is at home, ſo is the miniſter abroad*, [meaning the ſaid Don Carlos Martinez de Yrujo, the ſaid miniſter plenipotentiary and envoy extraordinary from His ſaid Catholic Majeſty, the ſaid King of Spain, to the United States] *The one* [meaning His Catholic Majeſty the ſaid King of Spain] *is governed like a dependant, by the nod of the five deſpots*
" *at Paris;* and *the other* [meaning the ſaid Don Carlos Martinez de Yrujo, the ſaid miniſter plenipotentiary from His ſaid Catholic Majeſty] *by the*
" *directions of the French Agents in America.   Becauſe thoſe infidel tyrants*
[The French Republic and their agents meaning] *had thought proper to*
" *rob and inſult this country and its government, and we have thought pro-*
" *per, I am ſorry to add, to ſubmit to it, the obſequious imitative Don* [The ſaid Don Carlos Martinez de Yrujo meaning] *muſt attempt the ſame; in*
" *order to participate in the guilt, and leſſen the infamy of his maſters.*"
[The French Republic and their agents meaning]

AND

AND ALSO; the faid WILLIAM did then and there, in the fame news-paper, and connected with the libel aforefaid, print and publifh the falfe feigned, fcandalous, and malicious, words and matters, according to the tenor following, to wit:

"In the prefent ftate of things, the independence of the United States is little more than a fhadow; it [the independence of the United States meaning] is really not worth what it coft to acquire and fupport it; and unlefs a ftop can be put to the progrefs of faction and foreign interference, [the interference of the faid Don Carlos Martinez de Yrujo, and the government of His faid Catholic Majefty meaning] inftead of a blefsing, it [the independence of the United States meaning] will 'ere long be a burden, which even the vaffals of Pruffia would not take off our hands as a gift."

AND the Grand Inqueft aforefaid, upon their oaths and affirmations aforefaid, do FURTHER PRESENT; that the faid WILLIAM COBBETT, being as aforefaid, and defigning and intending as aforefaid, On the twenty fourth day of July, in the year aforefaid, at the City and County aforefaid, wickedly and malicioufly did print and publifh, and caufe to be printed and publifhed, a certain other falfe, fcandalous, and malicious libel, of and concerning the faid Don Carlos Martinez de Yrujo, the faid minifter plenipotentiary and envoy extraordinary from the faid King of Spain to the faid United States, in the form of a communication, in which faid laft mentioned libel are contained, the falfe, fcandalous, and malicious matters and things, according to the tenor following, to wit:
"after fuch examples how can it be wondered at, that an advertifement fhould appear in our public prints, giving notice of a fwindling affignment of his eftate by a member of Congrefs, in the vicinity of the Capital, for the purpofe of defrauding his creditors, or that our people fhould join the French marauders, and pillage the property and threaten the lives of their defencelefs countrymen, under the flag of thefe pirates, or that we [the people of the United States meaning] are fo abufed and humbled as to fubmit with patience to the public infults of a frivolous Spaniard, half Don and half Sans-culotte." [meaning thereby the faid Don Carlos Martinez de Yrujo, minifter plenipotentiary and envoy extraordinary as aforefaid]

AND the Grand Inqueft aforefaid, upon their oaths and affirmations aforefaid, further do prefent, that the faid William Cobbett being as aforefaid, and defigning and intending as aforefaid, On the thirty firft day of July, in the year aforefaid, at the City and within the County aforefaid, wickedly and malicioufly did print and publifh, and caufe to be printed and publifhed, a certain other falfe, fcandalous, and malicious libel, of and concerning the faid King of Spain, and of and concerning the faid Don Martinez de Yrujo, the faid minifter plenipotentiary and envoy extraordinary of the faid King of Spain to the faid United States, in which faid laft mentioned libel, among other things, divers falfe, fcandalous and malicious matters are contained, according to the tenor following to wit:
—"What will his magnanimous majefty fay, when, by the refult of Don Yarico's [the faid Don Carlos Martinez de Yrujo meaning] confpiracy with Blount [meaning a confpiracy, or crime, for which WILLIAM BLOUNT, heretofore a Senator of the United States, was impeached by the Houfe of Reprefentatives of the United States, and expelled from the Senate thereof] and his appeal to the people, this political puppet [the faid Don Carlos Martinez de Yrujo meaning] fhall have brought on a war

E "with

" with America; when the standard of liberty shall be unfurled on the
" isthmus of Darien; then his Majesty [his said Catholic Majesty the
King of Spain meaning] may perhaps find, that the free born sons of Ame-
" rica are not that dastardly race of cowards, which the submission to the
" insults of his [the said King of Spain meaning] treacherous and piratical
" ally [the Republic of France meaning] had taught him to believe
" them;"—to the great scandal and infamy of his Catholic Majesty the
King of Spain, of his government, and the said Don Carlos Martinez de
Yrujo minister plenipotentiary and envoy extraordinary from his said Catholic Majesty the said King of Spain, to the evil and pernicious example of
all others in the like case offending against the act of assembly in such case
made and provided, and against the peace and dignity of the Commonwealth of Pennsylvania.

      JARED INGERSOLL,
         Atty. General.

WITNESS.

Hon. THOMAS M'KEAN, Esq.	sw. exd.
Dr. CHARLES CALDWELL,	sw. exd.
Dr. JOHN R. COXE,	sw. exd.
WILLIAM BRADFORD,	sw. exd.
WILLIAM MITCHELL,	sw. exd.
ISAIAH THOMAS,	sw. exd.
PATRICK DELANY,	sw. exd.
EZRA SERGEANT, at present in Virginia, therefore cannot be examined.	
STACY BUDD,	affirmed, exd.
ARCHIBALD BARTRAM,	affirmed, exd.

IGNORAMUS.

       William Coats, Foreman.

I, EDWARD BURD, Prothonotary of the Supreme Court of the Commonwealth of Pennsylvania, and Clerk of the Courts of Oyer and Terminer and general Goal delivery, holden before the Justices of the said Supreme Court for the said Commonwealth, hereby certify, that the fore-
going sheets contain a true Copy of a Bill presented to the Grand Jury, at
a Court of Oyer and Terminer and general Goal delivery, holden before
the said Justices, on the twenty seventh day of November last, for the
county of Philadelphia, and that the said bill was returned IGNORA-
MUS by the said Grand Jury.

    In witness whereof I have hereunto set my hand and
    affixed the seal of the said Supreme Court, at Philadel-
    phia, the seventh day of December in the year of our
    Lord MDCCXCVII.

         EDW. BURD, *Cl. Court.*

The following is a List *of the* Grand Jury.

LEFT SIDE.	RIGHT SIDE.
WILLIAM COATS,	FRANCIS GURNEY,
THOMAS FORREST,	ROBERT WHARTON,
PETER BROWN,	PETER MIERCKEN,
WILLIAM ROBINSON,	JOHN WHITEHEAD,
NATHAN BOYS,	DANIEL KING.
ISAAC FRANKS,	SAMUEL WHEELER,
ISAAC WORRELL,	JOHN C. STOCKER,
GEORGE LOGAN,	JOHN HOLMES,
WILLIAM PENROSE,	JACOB SERVOSS,
	ROBERT MORRIS.

This Bill of Indictment, however infignificant it may be in itfelf, has already made confiderable noife in the world, and it will yet make a great deal more. Papers of this fort generally travel from the court to the clerk's office; and there they lodge in eternal fleep. But this Bill is certainly deftined to another fate. Neptune will lend his waves and Æolus his winds to conduct it over the deep. It will fee climes that the inventors of it never faw, nor ever will fee. Little did they imagine, that they were becoming *authors*, and authors of fuch celebrity too, as, if it pleafe God, I will render them.

The identical copy of this precious document of liberty, which I received from the clerk's office, ftamped with the arms of poor Pennfylvania, I fhall fend to London by the next packet, addreffed to Mr. Reeves's loyal fociety of the Crown and Anchor. When they are infefted with the *reformifts*, or any other noify gang of *liberty men*, they will have nothing to do but ſhow them this Bill, and ſay: " Here, you dif- "contented dogs, is this what you are barking "after? If it be, go to that *free* country, Ameri- "ca. "I am much miſtaken if the bare ſight of it would not make more converts to their cauſe than all the means, that their talents and their laudable zeal have hitherto invented or employ- ed. It is a ſample of the liberty which the dif- affected in Britain are ſighing after; and they would exclaim with the old miller in the fable, "if ſuch is the *sample*, what muſt be the *sack*!"

The charges contained in the Bill of Indict- ment, lie buried in ſuch a multitude of words which mean nothing, or at leaſt nothing to the purpoſe, that they are very difficult to be under- ſtood. Some one ſays of a man extremely ver- boſe in his converſation, that "his wit is like three grains of wheat in a buſhel of chaff;" and exactly the ſame may with truth be ſaid of the meaning of this Bill. The *three libels*, as they are called, may all be contained in a quarter of a page, whereas the Bill is ſwelled out to three or four pages. Let us, then, ſift out the *three grains of wheat*, leaving the chaff behind.

The beſt way of doing this, and of enabling the reader to form a correct judgment both as to their import and their tendency, will be to lay before him the three publications (in which they are to be found) entire and undiſtorted, marking the pretended libellous parts in *italicks*.

1st.

From the Porcupine of 17, July, 1797.

For Porcupine's Gazette.

Ever since Spain has been governed by princes of the Bourbon family, the Spanish name has been disgraced, in peace and in war: every important measure has been directed by the crooked politics of France. This connection, like the obscene harpies of old, contaminates whatever it touches. But never has this been so conspicuous as in the present reign, and more especially at the present period. The degenerate prince that now sways the Spanish sceptre, whom the French have kept on the throne, merely as a trophy of their power, or as the butt of their insolence, seems destitute not only of the dignity of a king, but of the common virtues of a man: not content with allying himself to the murderers of a benevolent prince, who was the flower of his family, he has become the supple tool of all their most nefarious politics —As the sovereign is at home, so is the minister abroad, the one is governed, like a dependant, by the nod of the five despots at Paris, and the other by the directions of the French agents in America. Because those infidel tyrants had thought proper to rob and insult this country and its government, and we have thought proper, I am sorry to add, to submit to it, the obsequious imitative Don must attempt the same; in order to participate in the guilt, and lessen the infamy of his masters.——— Surely, if a revolution is ever to be recommended, it is when a prince thus entails ruin and disgrace on himself and his people, as Charles the 4th has done by this alliance with the regicide directory of France. Besides what she paid to purchase a dishonourable peace, Spain has already lost large sums in specie, a considerable part of her navy, and a very valuable island; and if she persist in her present stupid system of obedience, without claiming the second sight of a Scotchman, I will pronounce her ruin inevitable ——— Nothing is wanted but a conjoint operation between Great Britain and the United States, to open a way to all the riches of Mexico: and however Spain may deceive herself, it is not all the crooked manœuvres of French and American Jacobins, who are as much her enemies as ours, that can long prevent it. Events are pointing, with the clearness of a sun-beam, to the absolute, irresistable necessity of such a coalition. The base subsidised agents of France cannot long check the just resentment, or resist the measures of a high spirited and free people, who scorned to receive the law from freemen, and will never submit to receive it from slaves. The proud spirited of '76, that encountered dangers far more tremendous, than any that now present themselves, will burst not with the greater violence, for being so long restrained, and spreading from north to south will bear down all opposition.———The strength of this government is great, in its various resources, as well as in the affection of all its citizens, a few base profligates excepted; and nothing but the want of an union of councils, and an excessive love of peace, has hitherto prevented our enemies from feeling it. We hold the fate of the French and Spanish West-Indies in our hands; and without having recourse to the infernal practice of the French, the arming of slaves against their masters, we are able, with a small naval aid, to revolutionize all the kingdom of Mexico.——— But with all this respectability of strength and character, it has been the unhappy fate of this government to submit to violations and indignities, almost without example; and this has been owing as much to the tameness of its friends, as to the audacity of its enemies; for while these have been united and persevering, as all conspirators are, those have been torpid, and without any union or combination of efforts ——— In the present state of things the independence of the United States is little more

than

than a shadow: it is really not worth what it cost to acquire and support it; and unless a stop can be put to the progress of faction and foreign interference, instead of a blessing, it will ere long be a burden, which even the vassals of Prussia would not take off our hands, as a gift.——I remember what the tories prophecied at the close of the revolution war. "The prospect," said they, "that now looks so bright, will soon be darkened by clouds, heavier than any "that has yet hung over you. Your government will be torn by civil factions, "and you will be tossed to and fro, like a tennis-ball, by the contending na- "tions of Europe. France, which you now hug as an ally and equal, will "corrupt your citizens, and foment divisions among them; by which your go- "vernment will be so weakened that it will not dare to oppose her ambitious "designs. She can never forget her being expelled from this country with dis- "grace, nor will she fail to improve the first opportunity to recover some part "of it."——This is almost fulfilled in the present unfortunate state of things, but the case is not without a remedy, if prompt decision and firmness is adopted, on the part of government and its influential friends. To these the great body of the well-affected citizens look for an example. They feel the wounds of their country, they resent them, and if properly led would speedily avenge them. They fear neither the foreign enemy, nor the dastardly traitors among themselves, but would rejoice in an opportunity of sacrificing to both their much injured and insulted country.——In what consists the principal strength of France. It is in the poison of her principles among the mob, and corruption of her money among rebels and parricides. These have been the base diabolical arts, by which she has done as much as by her arms; and miserable has been the fate of all those countries, where they have been not seasonably and vigorously opposed. If after so many examples to teach us, we continue to fold our arms, and wrap ourselves up in an imagined security, our turn will come next: and we shall add one more to the gloomy catalogue of the tributatries of France.——Therefore let the friends of their country and its government associate at this critical juncture, to support the constituted authorities, and to oppose their enemies by spirited and united efforts. While traitors and foreign emissaries are daily insulting the chief magistrate by virulent and inflamatory publications; when the ministers of France and Spain, forgetting common decency, obtrude their appeals on the people, in order to mislead the ignorant; it is the duty of all those who condemn such criminal conduct to declare their resolution to oppose it.

An OLD SOLDIER.

2d.

From the Porcupine of 24, *July,* 1797.

COMMUNICATION.

AMERICAN MORALS.

To every reflecting mind, a review of the events which have taken place among some great political actors in the United States within a few years past; must be attended with extreme grief, mortification, and apprehension—with grief, for the great depravity and corruption of morals which they manifest;— with mortification, as they effect the honour and purity of the American character:—and with serious apprehension, of the consequences which may result from the influence of so many examples of an abandonment of integrity; not among the commonalty, for vice in the vulgar classes is to be met with every where;

where; but in high and exalted stations, and in persons selected by their fellow citizens to fill offices of great trust, distinction and confidence.——When we behold a secretary of state, in whom pride alone should have supplied the place of virtue, on account of the eminent and distinguished family from whom he was descended, and with whom he was related, basely forsaking his duty, meanly offering himself for a purchase, and bartering his country for the gold of an intriguing foreigner; when we see a great diplomatic character return from an embassy in which he betrayed the best interests of his country to the politics of an insiduous nation, and humbling the American people by listening to a public abuse of them, caressed, feasted, and justified by the first officers in the government; when a member of the senate of the United States is detected in debauching the fidelity of the public servants, and in plotting schemes of ambition and desperate enterprize, tending to commit the peace of his country; when it is now notorious that representatives of the people in Congress were instrumental in fomenting and encouraging the late insurrection in the west, and that the principles of the chief magistrate of the state in which it unhappily appeared, were so much suspected of disaffection, and his attachment to the country so questionable, that it was found unsafe to confide its suppression in his hands; when in fact, this very man, his family, and his friends, were discovered in applying to their own purposes, without form, and without security, large sums of money placed under the guardianship of a public institution; when the president and cashier of an extensive bank in the capital, and a principal officer in another bank in a great southern sea port, connected with a man not long since in an elevated situation, are found betraying their trusts, and embezzling the property they were paid to protect; when a judge of the pleas is publicly detected in shop-lifting; when an officer in a conspicuous station in the collection of the revenue is dismissed for delinquency; when a merchant, lately a member of the national legislature, the first some years past in a commercial character, has wantonly engaged in the wildest schemes of speculation and expence, and in connection with a man whose high reputation had called him to an elevated office of controul and superintendance, involving in their own fall, more families in general and pungent distress, than a thousand bankruptcies had ever produced; when an associate judge of the supreme court is held in duresse, for an immense debt, contracted in visionary plans of personal aggrandizement—when time has brought to light, that a profound philosopher and statesman, whose fame had filled Europe and America, meanly and traitorously consented, in the very moment of public enthusiasm, when these states had just atchieved their independence, to place IT in the hands of France, without condition, and without controul; in fine, when we view the second magistrate in the United States, the presiding head of an independent branch of the government, erecting the standard of opposition, rallying around it a host of malcontents, and taking a position as the chief of a faction; when we see him openly vindicating the insults and aggressions of a foreign nation, purposely misstating the political situation and sentiments of the country in correspondence with a distant stranger—and courted by the plunderers and enemies of America; when all these shameful and degrading circumstances are reviewed, what are we to think of our republican morals? Well may we exclaim with the confessor Fauchet "if this people are thus early decrepid, what may we expect "in their old age!"—The history of the most corrupt nation, and the most despotic or degenerate monarchy in Europe, cannot produce a like number of instances of such scandalous, criminal, and traitorous conduct in their public functionaries, it may be safely affirmed, even in the lapse of a century. *After such examples, how can it be wondered at, that an advertisement should appear in our public prints, giving notice of a swindling assignment of his estate, by a member of Congress in the vicinity of the capital, for the purpose of defrauding his creditors—or that our people should join the French m——ders, and pillage the property, and threaten the lives of their defenceless countrymen, under the flag of these pirates—or that we are so abused and humbled as to submit with patience to the public insults of a frivolous Spaniard, half Don and half Sans-Culotte?*

A. B.

3d.
From the Porcupine of 31. July, 1797.

From the GAZETTE of the UNITED STATES.

ANECDOTE.

From the BOURDEAUX "JOURNAL DES JOURNEAUX."

When the court of Madrid found itself compelled by the most imperious necessity, to make peace with the French republic, it was necessary to make the king sensible of the impossibility of continuing the war, and to resign himself to the sacrifices imposed by the treaty of peace. I thought, said the astonished monarch, that we had always beaten the French —*What will his magnanimous majesty say, when by the result of Don Yarico's conspiracy with Blount, and his appeal to the people, this political puppet shall have brought on a war with America. When the standard of liberty shall be unfurled on the isthmus of Darien; then his majesty may perhaps find that the freeborn sons of America are not that dastardly race of cowards, which their submission to the insults of his treacherous and piratical ally, had taught him to believe them.* And when Don Manuel de Godoy, Prince de la Paz, shall come before the magnanimous monarch, and with his finger in his mouth, tell him that it has become necessary to preserve the valuable mines of Peru, the extensive territory of Amazonia, Paraguay, Chili, and in short all South America, proper, by the surrender of all possessions, on this side the isthmus of Darien. It is much to be doubted if the monarch instead of tacitly admitting the argument of " imperious necessity," will not kick the sublime prince of peace from his presence, and turning his attention to the origin of so great evils, will allot a birth to Don Yarico in that commodious habitation where his respectable predecessor is so well accommodated; all the good he has done to Spain by *his translation of Smith's Wealth of Nations*, to the contrary notwithstanding.

These, reader, are the three publications, for which, under the *free* and *equal* government of Pennsylvania, I have been harrassed with a *criminal* prosecution; for which (besides the expence inseperable from all law concerns) I have been subjected to the infamy of an arrest, and have been dragged from my home, to the injury of my affairs and the great alarm of my wife and family.

I would not insult the respectable gentlemen, who composed the majority of the Grand Jury, or the good fenfe of the reader, by any attempt of mine to prove that nothing contained in thefe publications is of a libellous nature. If thefe are libels, there is no book facred or profane, which might not be conftrued into a libel. Every hiftory contains libel upon libel againft kings, queens and minifters. If thefe are libels, who is fafe? In fuch a ftate of things a man may draw down *the punishment of a murderer* on himfelf while he is faying his prayers or finging of pfalms.

Of the three publications, the two firft only *originated* in my Gazette: the other was taken from the *Gazette of the United States*, publifhed by Mr. Fenno. Of this latter circumftance I fhall fpeak more fully, when I come to the Chief Judge's charge.

The two publications, which made their firft appearance through my means, I have not the honour to be the writer of. They were both written by gentlemen of this city; *native* Americans, men who were determined *whigs* during the war for independence, republicans in principle, and firmly attached to the prefent government.

In the firft of thefe two publications, though there is certainly nothing libellous, I am ready to confefs there is a great deal of *warmth;* and if the admiffion of an effay extraordinarily warm, abounding in ftrong expreffions of refentment and, indignation, were ever juftifiable, they moft affuredly were on fuch an occafion. The commu-

F nication

nication of the OLD SOLDIER was sent me at a moment, when the city of Philadelphia, just quieted after the *appeal* of the French Minister Adet,* rang with the daring, the degrading, the contemptuous insult, which the Spaniard Yrujo had offered to the government of America and to every individual living under it.

He had published a most audacious letter to Mr. Pickering, the Secretary of State, containing a summary of all that is insolent. This letter had been handed and hawked about the city; and had, by his secretary, been sent to every public print for insertion. It was gone forth to the universe; and, that it tended to degrade and defame America, we need no other proof than the following paragraph from the London Gazette of the 14th of September.—
" The Americans are, according to our last advices from New-York, paying dear for their *independence.* The French take all their vessels, block up their very rivers, punish their seamen like malefactors, and actually make them pay for the shot they fire at them; while the Spanish Minister, with impunity, insults and braves their poor enfeebled government. He has written to Timothy Pickering, Esq. their first Secretary of State (see our Gazette of yesterday) in a language that Buonaparte would not venture to assume to his Cisalpine convention, or citizen Noel to the fallen and degraded Dutch: and what very much aggravates the insult, he has, without, permission from the President of the general Congress,
" communicated

* See Censor for November, 1796.

" communicated this letter to the people, as a
" fort of manifefto, or appeal, to them from
" their government. Nothing of this kind, we
" believe, ever before paffed *unresented,* except
" in a conquered or invaded country ; and we
" cannot help lamenting, that fo very little fpi-
" rit fhould be found in any people, but particu-
" larly in a people, who boaft their origin from
" Britons."

This paragraph, or at leaft the fubftance of it, I have feen in three London papers and in one Dublin paper ; fo that, it may be fairly concluded, its currency is by this time general, not only in the Britifh dominions, but all over Europe.—And, I pray, was no one to attempt to wipe away the ftigma ? Though the public papers had been made fubfervient to the fpreading of this deep fhame and difgrace abroad, was no printer to admit any thing that ferved to mark the ftrong indignation it infpired at home ? Was the prefs to be free for the Spaniard alone ? Was he to be allowed to taunt and threaten and defpife ; and were the poor Americans to few up their lips, or only mutter their impotent anger in fecret ? If this be fo ; if no man, by affuming a bold, an indignant, and retaliating tone, was to make an effort to refcue his country and himfelf from difhonour, without being harraffed with a profecution, without hazarding *the punishment of a murderer,* ours is a fallen ftate indeed ! If this be liberty and independence, or whatever elfe it may be called, God grant me the enjoyment of its oppofite. If this be freedom, may I be a bondfman, yea a very flave, to the end of my days.

"If fuch be juftice, fuch the laws,
"In the bleft clime where *Freedom* reigns,
"I gladly join the *tyrant's* caufe,
"And feek for refuge in my *chains*."

I fhall now come to Judge M'Kean's Charge to the Grand Jury; and fhall, without going out of court, take upon me to decide on its merits.

It was a charming thing this, for me to get hold of. I had long wifhed to poffefs fome fuch proof, fome fuch convincing proof, of the *fuperiority* of the American liberty of the prefs over that enjoyed in the "*Insular Bastile*," Great Britain; and it is to the defire that I have of giving it a portable and durable fituation, and to that alone, that this pamphlet is to be attributed: for which kind intention I humbly hope his *Honour* will feel inclined to pardon my paft mifdoings. His pretty *works* will now be read with admiration, in countries where, I am fure, had it not been for me, his name would never have once been articulated.

When this Charge, garnifhed with my fimple and good-natured comments, comes to be ferved up in Britain, it will be a difh for a king. The royalifts will lick their lips, and the republicans will cry, God blefs us! The emigration for *liberty's sake* will ceafe, and we fhall have nothing but the pure unadulterated dregs of Newgate and the Fleet; the candidates for Tyburn and Botany Bay. Bleffed cargo! All *patriots* to the back-bone: true philanthropifts and univerfal citizens; fit for any place but England in this world, and for heaven in the next.

The

The famous charge, which is to produce thefe excellent effects, was delivered to the Grand Jury at the Court of Oyer and Terminer, abovementioned in the Bill of Indictment. I fhall not fill up my pages in copying the former part of it, which the reader will, I am perfuaded, readily excufe when he has read the latter. Like two uncouth boorifh vifitants, the prefence of the one renders all apology unneceffary for the abfence of the other.

The Judge began, as, I believe, is ufual, with a definition of the feveral crimes, which generally fall under the cognizance of fuch a court: as, treafon, fodomy, rape, forgery, murder, &c. &c. But thefe his *Honour* touched flightly upon. He brufhed them over as light and trifling offences; or rather he blew them afide as the chaff of the criminal code, in order to come at the more folid and fubftantial fin of LIBELLING.

The weight, or rather the meafure, that his' Honour gave to this crime above all others, on this particular occafion, I fhall prove—not by ratiocination, but by arithmetic; by meafurement with the aid of a Carpenter's two-foot rule; as thus:

The Charge contains feparate definitions of 32 crimes, the whole of which, in the columns of the Gazette, occupy 5 F. 8 Inches, running meafure; of which that of LIBELLING alone occupies 3 F. 1 In. 6 P. On thefe dimenfions I ftate the following

PROBLEM.

PROBLEM.

If 32 Crimes occupy 5 F. 8 In. and 1 crime occupies 3 F. 1 In. 6 P. of how much greater magnitude ought this 1 crime to be than any 1 of the remaining 31.

SOLUTION—18 *Times.*

Thus, then, if we are to judge from the dimenfions of the Chief Juftice of Pennfylvania's charge, *Libelling* is eighteen times worfe, more dangerous and more heinous, than robbery, forgery, treafon, fodomy, or murder!

The fact is, the Charge feemed ftudied to excite a horror of no crime but that of libelling; the court feemed met for the punifhment of nothing elfe, and I feemed to be the fole object of that punifhment. Of this the reader will be convinced by a perufal of the Charge itfelf; and *the cause* he will find explained in the fubfequent remarks.

CHARGE.

The Chief Judge (M'KEAN), after having, as was before obferved, juft touched on the nature and punifhment of other crimes, proceeds, with refpect to LIBELS, thus:

> Before I conclude, *I am forry* to have occafion to mention, that there is another crime, that peculiarly concerns the judges of the fupreme court to endeavour to correct, it is that of LIBELLING. I will defcribe it at large.
>
> Libels or libelli famofi, taken in the moft extenfive fenfe, fignify any writings, pictures, or the like, of an *immoral* or illegal tendency; but in the fenfe we are now to confider them, are malicious defamations of any perfon, and efpecially of a magiftrate, made public either by writing, printing, figns or pictures, in order to provoke him to wrath, or to expofe him to public hatred, contempt or ridicule.

The direct tendency of thefe libels is the breach of the public peace, by ftirring up the objects of them, their families and friends to acts of revenge, and perhaps of bloodfhed; which it would be impoffible to reftrain by the fevereft laws, were there no redrefs from public juftice for injuries of this kind, which, of all others, are moft fenfibly felt; and which, being entered upon with coolnefs and deliberation receive a greater aggravation than any other fcandal or defamation, continue longer, and are propagated wider and farther. *And where libels are printed againft perfons employed in a public capacity, they receive an aggravation, as they tend to fcandalize the government*, by reflecting on thofe who are entrufted with the adminiftration of public affairs, and thereby not only endanger the public peace, as all others do, by ftirring up the parties immediately concerned to acts of revenge, but have alfo a direct tendency to breed in the people a diflike of their governors, and incline them to faction and fedition.

Not only charges of a heinous nature, and which reflect a moral turpitude on the party, are libellous, but alfo fuch as fet him in *a fcurrilous ignominious light*: For every perfon *defires to appear agreeable in life*, and muft be highly provoked by fuch ridiculous reprefentations of him, as tend to leffen him in the efteem of the world, and take away his reputation, which to fome men is more dear than life itfelf, for thefe equally create ill-blood, and provoke the parties to acts of revenge, and breaches of the peace.

A defamatory writing expreffing *only one or two letters of a name*, or ufing *fuch defcriptions and circumftances, feigned names or circumftances*, in fuch a manner, that *from what goes before*, and *follows after*, it muft needs be *underftood* to fignify fuch a perfon in the plain, obvious and natural *confruction* of the whole, is as properly a libel, as if it had expreffed the whole name at large: for it brings the utmoft contempt upon the law, to fuffer it's juftice to be eluded by fuch trifling evafions; and it is a ridiculous abfurdity to fay, that a writing, which is underftood by every the meaneft capacity, cannot poffibly be underftood by the courts and juries.

It is equally ridiculous and abfurd to fuppofe that if a man fpeaks flanderous or defamatory words of another, he may be fued, and ample damages recovered for the injury, but if the fame words are put in writing or printed, no punifhment can be inflicted. Such a doctrine may gratify the wifhes of envious and *malicious cowards and affaffins*, but muft be detefted by all fenfible and good men.

Thefe offences are punifhable either by indictment, information or civil action: But there are fome inftances where they can be punifhed by a criminal profecution only; as where the United States in congrefs affembled, the legiflature, judges of the fupreme court, or civil magiftrates in general are charged with corruption, moral turpitude, bafe partiality, and the like, when no one in particular is named.

By the law of the twelve tables at Rome, libels which affected the reputation of another, were made capital offences: But before the reign of Auguftus, the punifhment became corporeal only. Under the emperor *Valentinian, it was again made capital*, not only to write, but to publifh, or even *to omit deftroying them*. But by the laws of Pennfylvania, the authors, printers, and publifhers of a libel are punifhable *by fine*, and alfo a limited *imprifonment at hard labour*, and *folitary confinement in goal*, or *imprifonment only*, or *one of them*, as to the court in difcretion fhall feem proper, according to the heinoufnefs of the crime, and the quality and circumftances of the offender.

Any libeller, or perfon even fpeaking words of contempt againft an inferior magiftrate, as a juftice of the peace or mayor perfonally, though he be not then in the actual execution of his office, or of an inferior officer of juftice, as a conftable and fuch like, being in the actual execution of his office, may be bound to his good behaviour by a fingle juftice of the peace.

By

By this law and thefe punifhments, the liberty of the prefs (*a phrafe much uf'd but littl' underftood*) is by no means infringed or violated. The liberty of the prefs is indeed effential to the nature of a free ftate; but this confifts in laying *no previous reftraints* upon publications, and not in freedom from cenfure for criminal matter, when publifhed. Every freeman has an undoubted right to lay what fentiments he pleafes before the public; to forbid this, is to deftroy the freedom of the prefs; but if he publifhes what is improper, mifchievous or illegal, he muft take the confequences of his temerity. To punifh dangerous or offenfive writings which, when publifhed, fhall on a fair and impartial trial, be adjudged of a pernicious tendency, is neceffary for the prefervation of peace and good order, of government and religion; the only folid foundation of civil liberty. Thus the will of individuals is ftill left free, the abufe only of that free-will is the object of legal punifhment. Our preffes in Pennfylvania are thus free. The common law, with refpect to this, *is confirmed and eftablifhed by the conftitution itfelf*. By the 7th fect. of the declaration of the principles of a free government, &c. it is afcertained, " that the printing-preffes fhall be free to every perfon, who undertakes to examine the proceedings of the legiflature, or any part of government." Men, therefore, have only to take care in their publications, that they are decent, candid and true; that they are for the purpofe of reformation, and not of defamation; and that they have an eye folely to the public good. Publications of this kind are not only lawful but laudable. But if they are made to gratify envy or malice, and contain perfonal invectives, low fcurrility, or flanderous charges; they can anfwer no good purpofes for the community, but on the contrary, muft deftroy the very ends of fociety.—Were thefe to efcape with impunity, youth would not be fafe in it's innocence, nor venerable old age in it's wifdom, gravity, and virtue; dignity and ftation would become a reproach; and the faireft and beft characters, that this or any other country ever produced, would be vilified and blafted, if not ruined.

If any perfon, whether in a public or private ftation, does injury to an individual, or to the fociety, ample redrefs can be had by having *recourfe to the laws*, and the proper tribunals, where the parties can be heard perfonally, or by counfel, the truth can be fairly inveftigated, and juftice fully obtained: fo that there can be no neceffity nor reafon for accufing any one of *public* or private wrongs *in pamphlets or newfpapers*, or of appeals to the people, under *feigned names*, or by *anonymous fcribblers*.

Every one who has in him the fentiments of either a Chriftian or a gentleman, cannot but be highly offended at the envenomed fcurrility that has raged in pamphlets and news-papers, printed in Philadelphia for feveral years paft, infomuch that libelling has become a kind of national crime, and diftinguifhes us not only from all the ftates *around us*, but from the whole civilized world. Our fatire has been nothing but ribaldry and billingfgate: the conteft has been who could call names in the greateft variety of phrafes; who could mangle the greateft number of characters; or who could excel in the magnitude or virulence of their lies. Hence the honour of families has been ftained; the higheft pofts rendered cheap and vile in the fight of the people, and the greateft fervices and virtue blafted. This evil, fo fcandalous to our government and deteftable in the eyes of all good men, calls aloud for redrefs. To cenfure the licencioufnefs is to maintain the liberty of the prefs.

At a time when mifunderftandings prevail between the Republics of the United States and France, and when our general government have appointed public minifters to endeavour their removal and reftore the former harmony fome of the journals or news-papers in the city of Philadelphia have teemed with the moft irritating invectives, couched in the moft vulgar and opprobrious language, not only againft the French nation and their allies, but the very men in power with whom the minifters of our country are fent to negociate.

Thefe

These publications have an evident tendency not only to fruſtrate a reconciliation, but to create a rupture and provoke a war *between the ſiſter Republics*, and ſeem calculated to vilify, nay, to ſubvert all *Republican* governments whatſoever.

Impreſſed with the duties of my ſtation, I have uſed ſome endeavours for checking theſe evils, by binding over the editor and printer *of one of them*, licentious and virulent *beyond all former example*, to his good behaviour ; but he ſtill perſeveres in his nefarious publications ; he has ranſacked our language for terms of reproach and inſult, and for the baſeſt accuſations againſt every ruler and *diſtinguiſhed* character *in France and Spain*, with whom we chance to have any intercourſe, which it is ſcarce in nature to forgive ; in brief, he braves his recognizance and the laws. It is now with you, gentlemen of the grand jury, to animadvert on his conduct ; without *your aid* it cannot be corrected. The government that will not diſcountenance, may *be thought to adopt it*, and be deemed *juſtly chargeable with all the conſequences*.

Every nation ought to avoid giving any real offence to another. Some medals and dull jeſts are mentioned and repreſented as a ground of quarrel between the Engliſh and Dutch in 1672, and likewiſe cauſed Lewis the 14th to make an expedition into the United Provinces of the Netherlands in the ſame year, and nearly ruined that Commonwealth.

We are ſorry to find that our endeavours in this way have not been attended with all the good effects that were expected from them ; however we are determined to purſue the prevailing vice of the times with zeal and indignation, that crimes may no longer appear leſs odious for being faſhionable, nor the more ſecure from puniſhment for being popular.

The criminal law of this ſtate is ſo *pregnant with juſtice*, ſo agreeable to reaſon, ſo full of equity and clemency, that even thoſe who ſuffer, by it cannot charge it with rigor. It is ſo adapted to the common good as to ſuffer no folly to go unpuniſhed, which that requires to be reſtrained ; and yet ſo tender of the infirmities of human nature, and of the wives and children of even the greateſt offenders, as to refuſe no indulgence which the ſafety of the public will permit. It gives the rulers no power but of doing good, and deprives the people of no liberty but of doing evil. We are now (thank God) in the peaceable and full enjoyment of our laws, of the free adminiſtration of juſtice, and in complete poſſeſſion of religious, civil and political liberty. May the Divine Governor of the world continue theſe bleſſings to us, and impreſs it as a duty which we owe to ourſelves who enjoy them ; to thoſe virtuous men, who, under God, have been chiefly inſtrumental in procuring them ; and to our poſterity who will claim at our hands this nobleſt inheritance, to maintain and defend them at every hazard of life and fortune.

You may now, gentlemen, retire to your room. Inquire with zeal, hear with attention, deliberate with coolneſs, judge with *impartiality*, and decide with fortitude. And may God over-rule and direct all your proceedings to the furtherance of juſtice and the happpineſs of the people.

I have ever entertained the notion of an immediate ſuperintending Providence, and I moſt ſincerely believe, that God did over-rule and direct all the proceedings of this Grand Jury; for they did judge with *impartiality*, and decide with *fortitude*, though their judgement and deciſion were not *quite* conſonant to the wiſhes of the Chief

Chief Juſtice of Pennſylvania, as appeared not only from his Charge, but alſo from what he hinted repecting the Jury, the day after the Bill was returned.*

So pointed, ſo perſonal a charge, I am bold to ſay, was never before delivered from the Bench in any country, that has the leaſt pretenſions to civil liberty. If it be foreſeen, that a particular caſe, rather novel, is to come before a Grand Jury, it is the cuſtom for Judges, as it certainly is their duty, to explain its nature, its tendency, and the law reſpecting it fully and minutely; but never, till the 27th day of laſt November, did a Judge, preſiding to adminiſter juſtice according to the mild and impartial precepts of the Common Law of England, ſo far forget the genuine ſpirit of that law as to point directly at a ſingle offender, and to employ all the perſuaſion in his power to bring down chaſtiſement on his head.

The Charge contains every thing calculated to awaken the apprehenſions of the Grand Jury as to the effects of my conduct, and to prepoſſeſs their minds againſt my perſon. In every thing but elegance and animation, it was more like the zealous and impaſſioned pleadings of an advocate, than the calm, dignified, and impartial

---

* The day after the Bill was returned Ignoramus, the Chief Juſtice, on the trial of Mr. Humphreys for beating Bache, told the priſoner, that, if he had thought himſelf agrieved by the preſs, he ſhould have appealed to the law; and added; "you may ſay, indeed, that Gand Juries will not do *their duty;* we have had a *recent inſtance of that.*"——On this reflection on the Grand Jury, it is not my duty to comment. But, had I been one of the gentlemen who compoſed it, I think I ſhould have made an attempt, at leaſt, to defend my conduct and character.

partial accents that ever fhould breathe in the language from the Bench.

And, what was there, I pray, either in my character, in the particular cafe before the Grand Jury, or in the general tenor of my publications, to warrant this odious departure from the excellent rules, which had their origin in decency and candour, and which have been rendered facred by the practice of our fore-fathers? A ftranger, had there been one in court, would naturally have concluded me to be a notorious defamer of innocence, a feditious and turbulent troubler of the government, a fworn enemy of morality and religion; in three words, a profligate, a rebel, and a blafphemer.

It hardly ever becomes a man to fay much of his private character and concerns; but, on this occafion, I truft I fhall be indulged for a moment. I will fay, and I will make that faying good againft whoever fhall oppofe it, that I have never attacked any one, whofe private character is not, in every light which it can poffibly be viewed, as far beneath mine as infamy is beneath honour.—Nay; I defy the city of Philadelphia, populous as it is, and refpectable as are its inhabitants in general, to produce me a fingle man, who is more fober, induftrious or honeft; who is a kinder hufband, a tenderer father, a better mafter, a founder friend, or (though laft not leaft) a more zealous and faithful fubject.

Moft certainly it is unfeemly in any one to fay thus much of himfelf, unlefs compelled to it by fome public outrage on his character; but,
when

when the accufation is thus made notorious, fo ought the defence. And I do again and again repeat, that I fear not a comparifon between my character and that of any man in the city : no, not even with that of the very Judge, who held me up as the worft of mifcreants. His Honour is welcome, if he pleafe, to carry this comparifon into *all* the actions of our lives, public and *domestic*, and to extend it beyond ourfelves to *every branch of our families.*

As to my writings; I never did flander any one, if the promulgation of ufeful truths be not flander. Innocence and virtue I have often endeavoured to defend, but I never defamed either. I have, indeed, ftripped the clofe-drawn veil off hypocricy; I have ridiculed the follies and lafhed the vices of thoufands, and have done it fometimes, perhaps, with a rude and violent hand. But, thefe are not the days for gentlenefs and mercy. Such as is the temper of the foe, fuch muft be that of his opponent. Seeing myfelf publifhed for a rogue *and my wife for a whore ;* being prefecuted with fuch infamous, fuch bafe and hellifh calumny in the *philanthropic* city of Philadelphia, merely for afferting *the truth* refpecting others, was not calculated, I affure you, to fweeten my temper and turn my ink into honey-dew.

My attachment to order and good government nothing but the impudence of Jacobinifm could deny. The object, not only of all my own publications, but alfo of all thofe which I have introduced or encouraged, from the firft moment that I appeared on the public fcene to the prefent

fent day, has been, to lend fome aid in ftemming the torrent of anarchy and confufion. To undeceive the mifguided, by tearing the mafk from the artful and ferocious villains, who, owing to the infatuation of the poor and the fupinenefs of the rich, have made fuch a fearful progrefs in the deftruction of all that is amiable and good and facred among men. To the government of this country, in particular, it has been my conftant ftudy to yield all the fupport in my power. When either that government, or the worthy men who adminifter it, have been traduced and vilified, I have ftood forward in their defence; and that too, in times when even its friends were fome of them locked up in filence, and others giving way to the audacious violence of its foes.—Not that I am fo foolifhly vain as to attribute to my illiterate pen a thoufandth part of the merit that my friends are inclined to allow it. As I wrote the other day to a gentleman who had paid me fome compliments on this fcore, "I fhould never look at my family with "a dry eye, if I did not hope to outlive my "works." They are mere tranfitory beings, to which the revolutionary ftorm has given life, and which with that ftorm will expire.—But, what I contend for, and what nobody can deny, I have done all that laid in my power: all I was able by any means to accomplifh, in order to counteract the nefarious efforts of the enemies of the American government and nation.

With refpect to religion, though Mr. M'Kean was pleafed to number it among the things that were in danger from the licentioufnefs of the prefs, and, of courfe, from poor ME, I think it would

would puzzel the devil himself to produce, from my writings, a single passage, which could, by all the powers of perversion, be twisted into an attack on it. But, it would, on the contrary, be extremely easy to prove, that I have, at all times when an opportunity offered, repelled the attacks of its enemies, the abominable battalions of Deists and Atheists, with all my heart, with all my mind, with all my soul, and with all my strength. The bitterest drop in my pen has ever been bestowed on them; because, of all the foes of the human race, I look upon them, after the Devil, as being the greatest and most dreadful. Not a sacrilegious plunderer, from Henry VIII to Condorcet, and from Condorcet to the impious Sans-Culottes of Virginia, has escaped my censure. All those who have attempted to degrade religion, whether by open insults and cruelties to the Clergy, by blasphemous publications, or by the more dangerous poison of the malignant modern phisophy, I have ranked amongst the most infamous of mankind, and have treated them accordingly.

After this summary defence of my character and writings, the necessity of which I sincerely regret, justice demands that I should enter into an exposition of the unparalleled partiality that has been exercised towards me: and when I have done that, I pledge myself to prove, in contradiction to all the boastings which we have heard, that the press is free-er in Great Britain than in America.

To read the Chief Judge's famous Charge, one would inevitably be led to imagine, that no
person

perfon in this country, except PETER PORCUPINE, ever attempted to exercife the Liberty of the prefs, or even that pitiful portion of it which his Honour had the mercy to leave in our hands. All the other printers, one would think, had been poor paffive devils, and that their fheets had contained nought but vapid fongs of liberty, lying eulogies on departed rafcallity, and fulfome flattery of villains in power. But, to do juftice to my brother printers, to myfelf, and to Judge M'Kean, I am compelled to prove that this was not the cafe.

There are certain news-printers in this country, who may be counted as a fort of blanks: creatures that have nothing of humanity about them but the mere exterior form and motion, and that are, in every other refpect, as perfectly logs as if they had been cut out of a piece of timber. I will not degrade myfelf by a comparifon between my conduct and that of thefe dull, fenfelefs, inanimate beings. Let me have the fame privileges as other living active creatures, and I am content.

The reader has feen all that could be conjured up againft me in the Bill of Indictment, which he may fafely fet down among the moft virulent of my publications ; for lawyers and judges know very well how to fingle the tares from the wheat. But, I am willing to allow him a fcrutiny into every fentence I have written or publifhed, to which the Chief Judge's Charge can poffibly be made to apply, and then I will leave him to compare my " nefarious publications" with the " *decent, candid,* and " *true*"

" *true*" ones, which I am now about to produce from the preffes that have, and ftill do, efpoufe the caufe of the enemies of this country.

As libels againft *religion* are certainly more heinous in their nature, as well as more deftructive in their confequences, than any that can be publifhed againft men, however eftimable their characters or exalted their rank, I fhall firft take notice of a publication or two of this fort, which have efcaped the notice of the *vigilent* Chief Juftice of Pennfylvania : and this, I think, feems the more neceffary, as the Judge included *religion* among the objects endangered by the licentioufnefs of the prefs.

In the Summer of 1796, a work was publifhed by one Stephens (an Irifh Patriot, who has fince fpunged his creditors), entitled : " *Christianity contrasted with Deism* :" And, by a mafter-piece of bafenefs, before unheard of among the moft infamous of fcribblers, my affumed name, Peter Porcupine, was inferted in the title page, in order to give currency to the pernicious production.

This pamphlet abounded with the moft daring impiety ; and, though I will not take upon me to fay that the Chief Juftice ever *saw* it, he muft have heard of its exiftence ; for it was not only advertifed for fale, but there were alfo a confiderable number of paragraphs refpecting it, both in Bache's and Mr. Fenno's paper.

As to the Age of Reason, its publication, by Bache and others, is too notorious a fact to
be

be for a moment dwelt upon. This blafphemous work has been fpread all over the ftate, and through this city in particular.

BACHE has, for years paft, and does now, publifh and fell, what is called the " *Republican* " *Calendar*" ; in which the *Christian Æra* is fupplanted by that of the degrading Atheiftical Decadery of France.

All thefe publications, and many more that might be mentioned, have been, and yet are, publifhed in Pennfylvania. Their evident and inevitable tendency, is, to corrupt the young, miflead the ignorant, abafh the timid, degrade the prieft-hood, and, finally, to fubvert and deftroy, root and branch, the Chriftian Religion and all its ineftimable bleffings.

I have the fame opinion of the Judge's law knowledge that moft people have ; but he muft certainly know, that *Christianity* is part of *the law of the land*; that to deride and blafpheme it is punifhable by the common law ; and that it is the duty of all magiftrates, more particularly Judges, to make the law, in this refpect known, and to fee it executed.

Yet, in the ftate of Pennfylvania, under fo watchful a Chief Juftice, this falutary law, intended to preferve from indignity the religion of our forefathers ; to enforce a refpect for the laws of God, and to promote our eternal falvation, has been fuffered to fleep in oblivion; while the fanguinary *Twelve Tables of Rome* have been reforted to, in order to enhance the

H magnitude

magnitude of *the crime of satirizing the Spanish king and his minister!*—Gracious God! can the defcendants of Britons ever approve of this violence on *the common law of England?*

The Judge tells us that, with refpect to libels, the *common law* is *confirmed* by the *constitution of Pennsylvania;* and every one knows, that the common law of America is neither more nor lefs than the common law of England.—Now, it is well known, that the publifher of Paine's Age of Reafon has been profecuted in England; that Lord Kenyon termed it a "nefarious " publication, intended for the moft malignant " purpofes;" and that the jury inftantly found the defendant Guilty.—But England is, in this refpect, no more fit to be compared with America than Lord Kenyon is to be compared with *Judge* M'Kean.

I have been told, indeed, that the article of the conftitution, which provides for an entire freedom as to religious worfhip and opinions, forbids any reftraint on the prefs where fubjects of this fort are agitated. If this be true, and if M'Kean's doctrine of libels be alfo true, all that the American prefs has gained by the "Glorious Revolution," is, the horrid liberty of blafpheming the Almighty!

Quitting libels againft *religion*, let us come to thofe of a lefs horrid, though not lefs odious nature.

The Chief Juftice tells us, that "the *honour of* " *families* has been *stained,* and the greateft
" *services*

"*services* and *virtue* blafted;" and he before told us, that this evil it was *peculiarly the duty* of the Supreme Court to reprefs.

I have before obferved, and I repeat it again and again, that *innocence* or *virtue* was never attacked by me; and hence it is impoffible that I can ever have brought a *stain* on a family. Whether others have done this in Philadelphia, I leave the reader to judge from the following paffages of a pamphlet, publifhed here about two years and a half ago.

The fubject of the author's cenfure, is a debate in Congrefs. After calling one member an *Ass* and another a *Snap-Turtle*, he comes to a Gentleman of New-Jerfey, who now fills an office of great truft under the Federal Government, of whom and of whofe family he fpeaks thus : " Not that I would declaim againft
" Congrefs wages, for I think they ought to have
" at leaft ten dollars a day; otherwife an ho-
" nourable member from Jerfey will not be able
" to keep Mrs. B . . . . in town during the
" next feffion.*—Ten dollars, I think, will de-
" fray all expences—The honourable reprefen-
" tatives may then play cards and dice, and bil-
" liards, and do many other things——and
" Mrs. B . . . . may afford to *knock off a few*
" *bottles of Madeira* with fome of her foft *rosy-*
" *nosed visitors,* without finking her honourable
" fpoufe *forty shillings below par.*"

From members of Congrefs and their wives, the author comes to the Clergy and theirs. Few
people

* " See his fpeech in the Houfe of Reprefentatives."

people have forgotten, that, in 1795, a Sermon on National Gratitude was preached in this city, by a leraned Divine, then at the head of Princeton College. In the courfe of this much admired fermon, the preacher took occafion to cenfure the *Age of Reason* ; and this it was that brought on him, from our *decent* writer, the following attack : " Notwithftanding his confter-
" nation, he does not forget to bullyrag Tom
" Paine. Forty two miles did he trudge through
" thick and thin, Jonah like, to fave this our
" Nineveh by reading a fermon, and may hea-
" ven reward his labours ! May the fountains of
" Helicon gufh from his brains ;—And may all
" the curbers of the factious, fip nocturnal infpi-
" ration from the lips of the mufe of Morven,
" at the limped ftreams of Stony-brook, nor *be*
" *pestered with a d . . . . d wife* ;—May they ne-
" ver be dragged head-foremoft down the fteps
" of Naffau-Hall, *nor be pelted with brick bats*
" *and potatoes.*"

Is this " *decent, candid,* and *true*"? And, if it be not, how came it to " efcape with impuni-
" ty"? How came it not to attract the attention of the Supreme Court of Pennfylvania, whofe
" peculiar duty it is to reprefs and correct fuch
" exceffes"?—The book was publifhed in all the news-papers ; it was fold by all the bookfellers *except me* ; it was even hawked about the ftreets, and was the fubject of univerfal cenfure and abhorrence ; and yet the Supreme Court never did cenfure it ; nor did the Chief Juftice ever feel himfelf " impreffed with the duties of
" his ftation" to *bind the author or publifher over* !

The

The author was known to a *certain Secretary*; was even his intimate acquaintance and companion; and his pamphlet abounds with invectives *against Great Britain*, and high founding *compliments to France*. His politics, I suppose, he had the prudence to intend as a fort of atonement for his offences.

From the *staining of families* let us turn to the attacks of men in their public capacities.

The Chief Justice tells us, that, when defamatory writings are published " against persons " in a *public capacity*, they receive an *aggrava-* " *tion*, as they tend to scandalzie the government, &c. &c."

This doctrine, by-the-bye, I believe few men, except those in a public capacity will relish. It is exactly contrary to the spirit, as well as the letter, of the little pamphlet, entitled, " The Constitution of Pennsylvania."—In that inestimable performance, there is one Chapter containing a list of what are there called " the essential principles of liberty," which are positively declared to be excepted out of the general powers of government, and fixed on for ever to remain inviolate.—Among the precious things thus carefully preserved, is, *the liberty of the press*; and it is said, that no law shall be made to restrain any person, " who undertakes to ex- " amine the proceedings of the legislature " *or any branch of government*." And again it says, that, " in prosecutions for the publication
" of

" of any papers, inveſtigating the official con-
" duct of officers, or *men in a public capacity*,
" the truth thereof may be given in evidence."

Thus, you ſee, this pamphlet of Pennſylvania holds out to the world, that men in a public capacity are more open to the cenſure of the preſs than the ſovereign citizens are, which is, indeed, no more than reaſonable; but this Judge, this *learned* expoſitor of the law and conſtitution, tells us, that cenſorious writings receive an *aggravation*, when written againſt perſons in a *public capacity*!

However, be it ſo. Let us prefer the Judge's aſſertion to the declaration of the ſovereign people of Pennſylvania. Let us, for a moment, look upon their conſtitution as merely intended to amuſe them and the world; and then let us ſee what this State Government, and this ſame Judge, have permitted to paſs unreproved and unnoticed, in writers inimical to the Federal Government, and notoriouſly in the pay of France.

I could here produce volumes of the moſt attrocious calumny againſt the Federal Government and its officers individually; but, beſides my want of room, I am prevented by the notoriety of the fact. Every one in America knows what I have here generally ſtated, to be true; and it is therefore neceſſary to introduce only a few inſtances for the information of foreigners.

Bache, in his paper, No. 1037, after loading the Executive of the United States with various

rious falfe and infamous charges, fays: "And
" are we fo corrupted and debafed as to give up
" this precious jewel (Independence) to the in-
" trigues of *rascals* and *traitors*, who are about
" to *sell themselves and their country* ?"

This is pretty well for the Executive. Now
let us hear what CALLENDER (in his "Hifto-
" ry of the United States for 1796") fays of the
Congrefs in a lump—" If a man," fays he, "was
" to be kept a twelve month in irons, and then
" to be hanged for ftealing *one* horfe, what ought
" to be done with the Congrefs and their agents,
" who *forcibly pilfered* fo many that are yet un-
" paid for?"—I muft leave JUDGE M'KEAN to
anfwer this queftion; for he was, I believe, one
of the Congrefs that Callender alludes to.
However, left any offender fhould flip him, the
Historian takes care to include in his cenfure,
the fecond, the third, and the fourth Congrefs.

From the Government in general we will
now come to particular members of it.—The
Judge tells us, if publications, "containing per-
" fonal invectives, low fcurrillity, and flande-
" rous charges, were to efcape with impunity,
" the *fairest* and *best characters*, that this or any
" other country ever produced, would be vilifi-
" ed and blafted, if not ruined."

Now then, let us hear BACHE again; the
mouth-piece of the French faction, and fre-
quently the companion of the Chief Juftice at
Civic Feftivals.—This atrocious wretch, in his
paper of the 9th of July, 1795, has the following paragraph :—" The day" [the 4th of July]
"was

" was clofed by the exhibition of a tranfparent
" painting, with the figure of *John Jay* upon it.
" The figure was in full ftature, holding in his
" right hand a pair of fcales, containing in one
" fcale, *American liberty and Independence*, kick-
" ing the beam ; in the other, *British Gold*, in
" extréme preponderance. In his left hand a
" Treaty, which he extended to a group of Se-
" nators, who were grinning with pleafure and
" grafping at the Treaty. From the mouth of
" the figure iffued thefe words : *come up to my
" price, and I will sell you my country.* The fi-
" gure was burned at Kenfington amidft the ac-
" clamations of hundreds of citizens. Thus
" terminated the anniverfary of American In-
" dependence."

This recalls to our minds two valuable facts :
1ft, that this infamous libel did " efcape with
" impunity!" and 2d, that the exhibition and
actions which it records, did alfo " efcape with
" impunity ;" and that too in this city, under the
eye of this very Judge M'Kean And, what is
more, a gentleman, who, like a good citizen,
turned out of his bed to endeavour to put a ftop
to the fcandalous and difgraceful proceffion,
was affaulted in a moft cowardly and cruel manner, and never obtained the leaft fatisfaction.
Not one of the rabble, nor of the ring-leaders,
nor of the printers, who ftimulated them to action, and who recorded their atrocities as honourable deeds, was ever punifhed, or " *bound over,*"
or even reprimanded !—But this was a riot and
a libel againft a *worthy man*, an officer of the
Federal Government, and *no tool of France* ; and
thefe

thefe dircumftances muft account for what cannot otherwife be accounted for.

BACHE, in his paper, No. 1460, calls the Honourable John Jay, then Chief Juftice of the United States of America, and now Governor of the State of New-York: he calls this gentleman, " that *damned arch traitor* JOHN JAY."—And yet he was never " *bound over* ;" and yet he never was *personally attacked from the Bench;* but, on the contrary, has often, fince that time as well as before, fat at the fame board with the Chief Juftice!

I could here name at leaft one hundred of the greateft and beft men, that this country ever produced, who have been vilified by this reprobate defcendant of Old Franklin ; but, for the reafons before mentioned, I fhall forbear the enumeration, and content myfelf with an inftance or two of his attacks on the character of GENERAL WASHINGTON, for which every good man, in every part of the world, muft and will execrate the libeller and his fupporters.

He publifhed PAINE's letter to the GENERAL; of which he claimed an exclufive copy-right, and which he boafted of having received from Paris for the purpofe of publication. In this work, GENERAL WASHINGTON and the CONSTITUTION OF THE UNITED STATES, are both the objects of obloquy and reproach. The worthy old veteran and ftatefman, whofe endeavours have fo eminently contributed to the greatnefs and profperity of his country, is called, " the " *patron* of *fraud,*"—" an *imposter,* or an *apos-*
" *tate.*"

" *tate.*"—Yet the vile printer was never " *bound* " *over.*"

Thus was the city of Philadelphia difgraced. Thus did the Chief Juftice of Pennfylvania quietly look on, and obferve the propagation of a libel, that has excited univerfal indignation in the breafts of unconcerned foreigners, and for which both the writer and the printer are cenfured by their very partizans.

But, this was not the laft ftab that the literary aflaflin had in referve for the character of this great and good man, and for the honour of America.

The day that the GENERAL clofed his public labours (the 4th of March, 1797,) BACHE, after announcing his retirement from the Office of Prefident, fays : "If there ever was a period " for rejoicing this is the moment—every heart, " in unifon with the freedom and happinefs of " the people, ought to beat nigh with exultation, " that the name of WASHINGTON from *this day* " *ceases to give currency to political iniquity*, and " to *legalize corruption.*"

Yet, we are not at the worft : for, on the 13th of March, 1797, this viperous Grand Son of Old Franklin, accufed the fame eminent perfon of *murder* ! brought forward a long, formal, and circumftantial charge of cool, deliberate *afjaffination*, " *committed by* GEORGE WASHINGTON, " *late President of the United States.*"

The

The Chief Juſtice has *not forgotten*, I dare ſay, that I was the only printer in the United States (with ſhame be it ſpoken) who had the zeal and the induſtry to ſearch for the documents relative to the affair alluded to (which took place in 1753); to expoſe the falacy of the charge, and to hold the vile inſtrument of France up to univerſal abhorrence.

One would have thought, whatever might be the ſecret diſpoſitions of the Chief Juſtice of Pennſylvania, that outward appearances, common decency, would have led them to take ſome little notice of theſe outrages or a public and private character, reſpected, eſteemed, and revered by the wiſe and the virtuous of all nations. More eſpecially one would have expected this from a Judge, who now ſeems to be ſo anxious to preſerve the reputation of "*youth* in its *innocence*," and of "*old age* in its *gravity* and *wiſdom* ;" who now, in order to excite a horror againſt libelling, goes back to that cruel code, the *Twelve Tables of Rome*, and the no leſs ſanguinary laws of *Valentinian* ; who, in his zeal to make an example, does not think it derogatory to his honourable ſtation to point at a particular man, and call on the Jury, in expreſs terms, for their " *aid*" in his puniſhment ; and finally, who expreſſes his determination to purſue the vice of libelling with " zeal and indignation." From ſuch a Judge, who would not have expected an interference ; who does not believe, who does not know, and does not ſay, that he ſhould have been " *impreſſed with the duties of his ſtation,*" when the reputation of the Federal government was daily and hourly attacked in

his

his prefence; when the fame and character of GENERAL WASHINGTON were bleeding at every pore, and when the French printer BACHE and his coadjutors were purfuing the Aged Veteran to his domeftic retreat with all the hellifh malignity of Parifian cannibals?—Yes, this was the time for him to be "*impressed with the duties of his station.*" This was the time for him to exert his authority of *binding over;* to unfold and enforce *the severity of the law*, and eftablifh his character for *impartiality*:—but, this time is paft.

Thus have we feen the Chief Juftice of Pennfylvania wink at the moft daring and wicked libels, againft God and againft man, that a writer can conceive or a printer can print. But, we are not yet come to what may be properly called *a case in point*.

I was profecuted for publications levelled againft a foreign prince, government, and minifter; to form therefore a juft eftimation of the conduct and motives of thofe who urged the profecution, we muft take a fketch (and a very flight one will ferve) of what other printers have publifhed, *with impunity*, againft other governments, nations, and princes.

But, before I enter on this fubject, I think myfelf called on to make a few remarks on that part of the Judge's Charge, which dwells, with fuch emphafis and feeming dread, on the danger of offending foreign nations and potentates, particularly the *tender-hearted* rulers of France and the king of the country of the *Inquisition*.

After

After telling the Grand Jury, that I had
" ranfacked our language for terms of reproach
" and infult againft every *diftinguished* character
" in *France and Spain*," he tells them, that,
" without their aid," my conduct cannot be corrected, and concludes by obferving, that " the
" government that will not difcountenance, may
" be thought to adopt it, and be deemed *juftly*
" *chargeable with all the confequences.*"—Then
follow an inftance of the great danger of offending foreign nations in this way: the Judge refers to hiftory above a hundred years back, and
very gravely tells the Grand Jury, that " Some
" medals and dull jefts are mentioned and repre-
" fented as a ground of quarrel between the En-
" glifh and Dutch in 1672, and likewife caufed
" Lewis the 14th to make an expedition into the
" United Provinces of the Netherlands in the
" fame year, and nearly ruined that Common-
" wealth."

This was an example *in terrorem*, and was
evidently cited for the purpofe of impreffing on
the minds of the Jury, the peril that their country might be placed in from fuffering me to
" efcape with impunity." But, granting for a
moment, that laying a reftraint on the prefs,
*far fear the effects of its freedom should offend
foreign powers*; allowing that fuch an act is not
to the laft degree fhameful and debafing, and
only fuited to a country in the moft abject ftate
of vaffalage ; allowing this, let us fee if the
Judge's quotation was quite correct and candid.

Now, I fay, and every one of the moft fuperficial reading knows, that the *medals* and *dull
jefts*

jests alluded to, never were, nor are they any where (except in this learned Charge) " mention- " ed and *represented* as a ground of quarrel be " tween the Englifh and Dutch in 1672," nor at any other period. HUME, who, it will hardly be- denied, is at leaft as good an authority as Penn- fylvania's Chief Judge, does indeed fay, that " certain medals and pictures were made the " *miserable pretext* of a moft fcandalous breach " of faith," on the part of the profligate Charles II ; but he tells us that the *real grounds* of the war, were, the inordinate ambition of Lewis XIV, and the thirft for riches and arbitrary power of the corrupted miniftry of England, well known by the name of the CABAL.

Befides had medals and dull jefts really been, as they were not, the grounds of the war, can- dour fhould have led the Judge to continue his reference to hiftory a little further, and to tell the Grand Jury *how that war terminated,* and how the *nearly ruined Commonwealth behaved* with refpect to the medals and dull jefts.

Lewis XIV did, indeed, make a devaftating and cruel expedition into the Netherlands, and reduced the Dutch to the laft extremity by land, while the combined fleets of England and France nearly blocked up their ports and ruined their commerce. In this awful ftate of their affairs, the two unprincipled Monarchs made known to them their pretenfions, which, among many other humiliating terms, fpecified, that " all perfons " guilty of writing *seditious libels* againft them, " fhould, on complaint, be banifhed for ever " from the States."--The Commonwealth, though,

as the Judge fays, *nearly ruined*, fcorned the infolent pretenfions ; and, following the example of the PRINCE OF ORANGE (afterwards our WILLIAM III, of glorious memory) nobly refolved "to refift the haughty victors, and to de-
" fend thofe laft remains of their native foil,
" of which neither the irruptions of Lewis, nor
" the inundation of waters, had as yet bereaved
" them. Should even the ground fail them on
" which they might combat, they were ftill re-
" folved not to yield the generous ftrife ; but,
" flying to their fettlements in the Indies, erect
" a new empire in thofe remote regions, and
" preferve alive, even in the climates of flavery,
" that liberty of which Europe was become un-
" worthy."

This is what Mr. M'Kean fhould have told the Grand Jury ; and, he fhould have told them befides, that this brave refolution of the Dutch met with a glorious reward ; that a few months faw their gallant fleet a match for thofe of the two monarchs united, and that the haughty king of France, driven by the PRINCE OF ORANGE from fortrefs to fortrefs and from Province to Province, at laft entered his vain and frivolous capital covered with defeat and difgrace, before the triumphal arch of St. Dennis, erected for the celebration of his conquefts, was completely out of the hands of the architect !

This is the paffage of hiftory, which, above all others, the republican ear dwells on with pleafure ; this is what the Chief Judge fhould have related to the jury ; but, this would not have anfwered his purpofe. Such an example
of

of republican fortitude and heroifm would have founded well from the lips of his Honour; but, the Grand Jury of Philadelphia fhowed by their righteous decifion, that they ftood not in need of examples from hiftory to ftimulate them to act agreeably to the dictates of their confcience, and to reject with difdain every idea of fear, that their acquitting an innocent man might bring down on themfelves and their country the chaftifement of foreign nations.

Before I conclude my remarks on this part of the Charge, I cannot refrain from noticing the very odious impreffion it is calculated to give the world with refpect to the government, and the character of the American nation.

It is well known, that, at the time when the paragraphs againft Spain and France were publifhed, and when the charge was delivered, the former nation was in the open violation of their treaty with this country, which had juft then been grofsly infulted by their minifter; and that the latter were plundering its commerce in every part of the world, blocking up its rivers, lafhing its fea-faring citizens like convicts, and driving its humble negociators from their capital with fcorn and reproach. Thefe circumftances taken into confideration, what muft foreigners infer from the Charge? Will they not fay, and very juftly too : ' fuch is your *liberty of the* '*press*, fuch your *boafted independence*, that, let ' a nation trample on your rights, deride, infult, ' rob, and torture you, and your government ' ever ftands ready to inflict *the punishment of a* ' *murderer* on the firft man, who, in refenting
' your

' your injuries, shall step one inch beside the
' line of the labyrinthian law of *conſtructive*
' *libels*; and this cruelty it condescends to, left
' its lenity to its friends and supporters should
' give umbrage to an insolent and perfidious
' foe!'—Yes; this will they say; and if there
be an American, who can patiently bear the
disgraceful imputation; I admire his Christian
humility; but I envy him not his *liberty*, his
independence, or his *republicanism*.

After all, allowing that America is so beggared in means and so humbled in spirit; allowing these *independent* states to be already reduced to a pitch of general vassalage, that renders such a sacrifice to the pride and insolence of foreign nations prudent and necessary; allowing that the Judge made all this appear to be true, let us return, and see what the printers *of the French faction* have published against other governments, nations, and princes, without his feeling himself " impressed with the duties of his sta-
" tion," to *bind them over*.

Now, reader, prepare yourself for a catalogue of the most indecent, blackest, and most infamously libellous expressions, that ever dropped from the lips or pen of mortal man. The French language is very weak and steril compared to ours, particularly in terms of reproach and abuse. Their rascals spend their breath for half an hour in noisy volubility, to produce a faint idea of what ours can express in one short grind of the teeth. But, all this bitterness, all the force and fury, of this our dear mother tongue, the crafty Gaul has, we are now about to

fee, had the addreſs to bring over into his own
ſervice.

To begin with Callender: this little reptile, who, from outward appearances ſeems to have been born for a Chimney ſweep, and to be now following the ſooty trade, made his eſcape from the hands of Juſtice in Scotland, in the year 1793, after being apprehended as the author of a libellous pamphlet, entitled "*The Political Pro-*
"*gress of Britain.*"

This work, which is of conſiderable bulk, is nothing but a ſtring of falſhoods, interſperſed with the moſt audacious libels on the Britiſh miniſtry, and every branch of the Royal Family, which latter the author calls, the "*ruffian*
"*race of British Kings.*"—In one place he calls the Right Honourable William Pitt, a *hardened Swindler*, and in an other, he calls His Royal Highneſs the Prince of Wales *a murderer.* He, in one ſhort ſentence, conſigns to infamy both the Royal Family and the people at large.
" Since the Norman Conqueſt," ſays he, " Eng-
" land has been governed by thirty-three ſo-
" vereigns; and, of theſe, two thirds were, each
" of them by an hundred different actions,
" *deserving of the gibbet;* and *the people* ſeem to
" have been as perfectly diveſted of every ho-
" nourable feeling, *as Majesty itself.*"

Well, this pamphlet, though abounding in ſuch atrocious libels as theſe, and though the author in his preface, boaſts of having been obliged to fly from his country for publiſhing it, was republiſhed in Philadelphia, and was never *discountenanced*

countenanced by the government or the Chief Juſtice. Nay Callender ſays, in his preface, that *certain gentlemen*, and particularly *Mr. Jefferson*, the Vice Preſident of the United States, had *encouraged him* to give an American edition of this infamous performance!

I have a dozen ſources to which I could apply for libels againſt foreign princes and ſtates. Brown has been guilty of crimes of this kind without number, and ſo have Dunlap and his ſucceſſors. The Claypooles, no longer ago than September laſt, calls Her Majeſty the Queen of Portugal a *Crazy Lady* and a *Lunatic.* Oswald, to the day of his death, publiſhed at leaſt forty libels regularly, two days in a week ; but he is dead; I ſhall therefore leave him, and come to Bache, the Chief Judge's companion at Civic Feſtivals.

There is not a prince or power of Europe, who has diſcovered the leaſt inclination to oppoſe the French, or diſcredit their infamous principles, whom this caitiff printer and his ſupporters have not libelled in the moſt outrageous manner.—The Emperor of Germany and his generals have been called *thieves* and *scoundrels* a thouſand times ; the King of Pruſſia, *before his defection*, was called a *Sharper ;* the Empreſs of Ruſſia, in No. 1361, is called a *She-Bear.* But, the Britiſh nation, government, and king, have been the conſtant objects of their moſt wicked calumnies. Mr. Smith of Baltimore, in open Congreſs, called the King of Great Britain, " *a* " *monster ;* a *king of sea-robbers."* His ſhort ſpeech was publiſhed in all the papers of that day.

day. BACHE, in his paper, No. 1036, fays of Britain, that " *dishonour* mark her *councils and* " *her actions.*" In 1041, he calls the Britifh a " *perfidious nation.*" In 1081, he calls Britain, " that proud tyrannical and *infamous* kingdom." In 1083, he calls the people of Great Britain, " the *bloody savage islanders.*" The government, in various papers, he calls, " that *corrupt mo-* " *narchy*"—" that *corrupt government,*"—" a mix- " ture of *tyranny, profligacy, brutallity,* and *cor-* " *ruption.*"—In the letters of Franklin, publifh- ed in his paper, he calls Admiral Murry " *free-* " *booter* Murray."—In 1033, he calls His Britan- nic Majefty, " a *prince of robbers.*" In 1048, he calls him, " that prince of *land and sea rob-* " *bers,* GEORGE III." In 1031, he fays, fpeak- ing of Great Britain, " I pledge you my word, " that I fhould heartily rejoice, if *the Royal Fa-* " *mily,* were *all decently guillotined.*" And, final- ly, not to tire my readers with the abominations of this atrocious mifcreant, he puts a *mock speech* into the mouth of the king of Great Britain, and makes him conclude, as *under the gallows at Tyburn*!

Here are infults, if you talk of infults, to fo- reign nations. Nor are thefe the worft. A pam- phlet once before quoted, called a *Rub from Snub,* has the following " *decent*" lines; I will not call them verfes.

> " God fcourge Old England's king,
> " To earth the direful fpring
>   " Of tears and blood;
> " May *all fuch rafcals fall,*
> " *Lords, dukes,* and devils all,
>   " Biting the mud."

"When *Britains boaft* shall !e
"Difrob'd of royalty,
        "Difcord fhall fly
"But while *the monfter's* jaws
"Fix'd at her vitals gnaws,
        "Freedom fhall die."

"Why fhould Columbia's fire,
"Her ancient flame expire,
        "While nations rife?
"Still the *Brute Royal* raves,
"Unchains his *Britifh flaves*
        Fierce in your eyes.

"Why did juft heaven ordain
"*Kings* and their *mifcreant train*,
        "Pefts to this world?
"Deep in hell's ruthlefs flame,
"Shrouded in endlefs fhame,
        "May they be hurl'd."

Was there ever fuch abominable outrage as this offered to mortal man any where but in America? No; fince the art of writing was difcovered, there never were fuch libels tolerated againft any human being, whether friend or enemy. Yet, neither the government of Pennfylvania, nor the Chief Juftice, nor any other perfon in authority, ever interfered. No one, amongft all thefe libellers, was ever profecuted or *bound over*. Their *politics were perfectly French*, and all went fmoothly on.

Let us for a moment fuppofe (which, however, we have no right to do), that the ftupid and
                                    ungenerous

ungenerous prejudice prevailing againſt Great Britain, formed ſome trifling excuſe for the remiſsneſs (to give it the mildeſt term) of the executive and judiciary of the ſtate. Still, this could not apply to the libels publiſhed againſt other nations and princes; ſome of which had, and now have, *treaties af amity* with this country, and others were not, nor ever had been, its foes.

Amongſt theſe nations there is one, the libels againſt which I have reſerved for this place: I mean *Spain*. For three long years the King of Spain, his government and miniſtry, were the ſubject of conſtant abuſe and defamation. BACHE, in No. 1028 of his vile paper, ſays, "the "*ſlaves of Madrid* will ſoon ſhrink from the con- "querers of Toulon." And in No. 1044, he has, ſpeaking of Spain, theſe words: "The "*most cowardly of the human race;*"—"the *Spa- "niſh slaves ;*"—" the ignorant ſoldiery of the "*infamous tyrant of Castille.*"

Now, this is the very ſame Prince, and the ſame people, that I have been proſecuted for libelling. Compare what I have ſaid, or rather what I have publiſhed, concerning them; compare the paſſages in the Bill of Indictment with thoſe here quoted, and then praiſe the impartiality and juſtice *of the free and equal government of Pennsylvania*! *Don Yrujo* never thought the honour of his Maſter, when called an *infamous tyrant*, merited his zeal to defend it; nay, the very printer, who thus defamed him, the DON has employed as the printer of his *insolent letter to Mr.* PICKERING! This man's conduct is hardly worth notice; but how shall we account for the conduct of the Chief Judge of Pennsylvania? Surely the king of Spain's character ought to have been an object of his attention *then* as well as *now* ; unless we are willing to allow, that no character is under the protection of the laws of Pennsylvania, unless it be of *persons devoted to the will of France.*

But, before I conclude this comparison between what I have been most rigorously prosecuted for doing, and what others have done with impunity, I shall give the reader a specimen or two of the conduct of the officers of this Pennsylvania Government *(not excluding the Chief Judge himself)*, towards foreign nations and princes.

The Governor (Mifflin), assisted at a civic festival, when the following toasts were drunk; which were published in most of the news-papers.*

"Those *illustrious citizens* sent to *Botany Bay*. May they be *speedily recalled* by their country *in the day of her regeneration.*"

"May the spirit of Parliamentary reform in Britain and Ireland *burst the bands of corruption, and ov.rwhelm the foes of liberty.*"

"The *Sans-culottes* of France. May the robes of *all* the *Emperors, Kings, Princes,* and *Potentates* [not excepting the *king of Spain*], now employed in suppressing the flame of liberty, be cut up to make breeches."

This is pretty "*decent*" in a *Governor* ; but, without stopping to remark on the peculiar *decency* of his toasting a gang of *convicts*, let us come to another instance of his conduct, full as "*decent*" as this.

At

* See BACHE of 11 Feb. 1795.

At the civic feftival, held in this city in 1794, to celebrate the dethronement of " Our great " and good ally, Louis XVI," there were " af- " fembled," according to the *procés verbal*, which was fent to the Paris Convention, " the CHIEFS, " *civil and military*, of the State of Pennfylva- " nia."—The *procés verbal* contains a letter to the Convention, in which the following honourable mention is made of the Governor. " The " governor of Pennfylvania, that *ardent friend* " *of the French republic*, was prefent, and par- " took of *all our enthusiasm, and all our senti-* " *ments.*"

I believe they fpoke truth; for the cannons of the State were fired, and military companies, with drums beating and colours flying, attended the execrable fête, one of the ceremonies of which, was, *burning the Englifh flag*; and as to the *sentiments*, contained in the *oaths* and *speeches* (for there were both), they abounded in infults towards almoft all the princes of the earth, but particularly the king of Great Britain.

M‘KEAN dwells with great ftrefs on the danger to be apprehended from infulting foreign nations, more efpecially thofe with which we have *negociations pending*, and the *persons with whom we are to treat*. Well then, all the libels that I have here produced, againft His Britannic Majefty, his minifters, and his people; and this " *decent*" conduct on the part of " the CHIEFS, *civil and military*, of Pennfylvania," and on the part of the Governor himfelf; all thefe libels were publifhed, and this conduct took place, *at the very time, when* MR. JAY *was in England negociating*

negociating an amicable adjustment of differences, with the British ministry and their Sovereign!

The Chief Juftice, would, I dare fay, be very angry not to be thought included among " the " CHIEFS *civil* and military of the State of Penn- " fylvania ;" but I fhall leave nothing to *inference or suppofition*. Facts are what I love, and happily his conduct and character is not in want of plenty to illuftrate them. I could mention one civic feftival at which he affifted, where a " *revolution in Great Britain*" was toafted ; and another, where a toaft was, " *Succefs to the Uni-* " *ted Irishmen,*" then in open rebellion againft their king ; but, thefe would not, in point of time be quite to my purpofe : I fhall, therefore, come to one inftance of his conduct that is fo. It is a fort of companion piece to his Charge, and it fhall, for that reafon, be put exactly upon a parallel with it.

Judge M'Kean's Charge,
AGAINST
PETER PORCUPINE.

" At a time when mifun- " derftandings prevail between " the Republics of the U- " nited States and France, " and when our general go- " vernment have appointed " public minifters to endea- " vour their removal and re- " ftore the former harmony " fome of the journals or news- " papers in the city of Phila- " delphia have teemed with " the moft irritating invec- " tives, couched in the moft " vulgar and opprobrious lan- " guage, not only againft the " French

Peter Porcupine's Charge,
AGAINST
JUDGE M'KEAN.

At a time when mifunderftandings prevailed between this country and *Great Britain*, and when the General Government had appointed *Mr. Jay,* and fent him to England to endeavour to remove them, many news-papers and pamphlets in this city of Philadelphia, teemed with the moft falfe, moft vile, and moft rafcally abufe, not only againft the Britifh nation and their allies, but alfo againft the very minifters, and the very monarch, with whom he was fent to

"French nation and their allies, but the very men in power with whom the ministers of our country are sent to negociate. Thefe publications have an evident tendency not only to fruftrate a reconciliation, but to create a rupture and provoke a war between the fifter Republics, and feem calculated to vilify, nay to fubvert all *Republican* governments whatfoever.

"*Impreffed with the duties of my ftation,* I have ufed fome endeavours for checking thefe evils, by binding over the editor and printer of one of them, licentious and virulent, beyond all former example, to his good behaviour; but he ftill perfeveres in his nefarious publications; he has ranfacked our language for terms of reproach and infult, and for the bafeft accufations againft every ruler and diftinguifhed character in France and Spain, with whom we chance to have any intercourfe, which it is fcarce in nature to forgive; in brief, he braves his recognizance and the laws. It is now with you, gentlemen of the grand jury, to animadvert on his conduct; without your aid it cannot be corrected. The government that will not difcountenance, may be thought to adopt it, and be deemed juftly chargeable with all the confequences."

to treat. Thefe publications had an evident tendency, not only to fruftrate a reconciliation, fo neceffary to the peace, profperity, and happinefs of America, but to provoke a deftructive war between the two nations; and were, befides, calculated to vilify, and fubvert all *lawful* and *good* government whatfoever.

Yet, THOMAS M'KEAN, the Chief Juftice of Pennfylvania, *never was impreffed with the duties of his ftation,* fo far as to ufe any the moft feeble endeavour for checking thefe evils. He never did punifh, or profecute, or bind over, or reprimand, one of the infamous authors, printers, or publifhers; but on the contrary, when the unratified treaty was promulgated, he appeared at the head of a committee in the State-Houfe yard, furrounded with a vaft concourfe of rabble, affembled for the evident and avowed purpofe of preventing its ratification. Here *Hamilton Rowan* was, on motion from the chair, welcomed with many cheers; the rabble were called on to kick *the damned treaty to hell,* and they afterwards went and burnt it, with every mark of hatred and infult, *oppofite the door of the Britifh Embaffador!*

There

There is the text, reader: make the comment yourſelf; for I have not language to do juſtice to the indignant feelings that it excites in my breaſt.—Sum up the evidence, and judge of the candour and impartiality of the Chief Juſtice of Pennſylvania. All that could be conjured up againſt me, was included in the Bill of Indictment, the very harſheſt expreſſion to be found in which, is, my calling the king of Spain a " *de-* " *generate Prince* :" while I have proved, from papers and pamphlets now in print, and to be come at by every one, that others have printed, and publiſhed to the world, that Mr. Jay is a " damned arch traitor ;" General Waſhington a " patron of fraud, a legalizer of corruption, and " an aſſaſſin ;" that the Empreſs of Ruſſia is a " ſhe bear," the king of Pruſſia " a ſharper," the Queen of Portugal a " lunatic," the Prince of Wales a " murderer," the king of Great Britain a " brute, a monſter, a raſcal, and a robber, " worthy of the gibbet ;" and, laſtly, that the king of Spain, whom I only called a degenerate prince, has been boldly declared to be " an in- " famous tyrant!"—And, I again and again repeat, that the Chief Juſtice has ſuffered all this to paſs immediately under his ſight, unproſecuted, unreproved, and unnoticed ; while my publications have been watched with a never-ſlumbering eye, and proſecuted with a rigour unparalleled ; while two thirds of a charge to a Grand Jury have been directly pointed at my perſon ; while every ſevere maxim of our own law has been fought out ; and, as if all this were not enough, while the bloody twelve tables of Rome and the laws of Valentinian have been reſorted to, in order to excite a horror of

my

my offence, and to draw down punifhment on my head, for publifhing what an enlightened and honeft Grand Jury has determined, *not to be libellous*!

How difficult foever the reader may here find it to reprefs the emotions, which fuch hitherto unheard of conduct is calculated to excite, I muft beg him not to indulge them, 'till I have drawn his attention to a fact, which, in the crowd of matter, I dare fay has efcaped him.

I have amply proved, that the pretended libels, for which I have been profecuted, are to the real ones, publifhed by others, what the glare of a taper is to a city in flames. I have proved that the very monarch, whom I termed a " de-" generate prince," has been, by others, proclaimed as " an infamous tyrant." But, there was yet one fact wanting to render this fcandalous profecution complete; and that fact is at hand.

The reader, by turning back to page 36, will perceive, that one of my "falfe, fcandalous, and " malicious libels," as they are moft falfly and fcandaloufly called, did not originate with me, nor in my paper. It was copied from Mr. FENNO's paper *of an anterior date*. This material circumftance was, very cautioufly and *candidly*, kept *out of the Bill of Indictment*, though the heads and titles of the other two publications were mentioned; and there is every reafon to believe, that it efcaped the attention of the Grand Jury.

The

The Indictment, as is ufual, concludes with ftating the tendency of the crime, part of which is, " the *evil example* of all others in the like " cafe offending." This is moft certainly very proper : for, to prevent the effects of *evil example*, is, or ought to be, the principle object of all punifhments. But, how could I be faid to fet the *evil example*, when it was notorious that I had been far furpaffed by others, who had never been called to account, and when the very publication, for which I was profecuted, I had copied, word for word, from another printer, a native of the country, and living in the fame city with myfelf? Mr. FENNO has never been *bound over*. He has never been arrefted : nor has he been even fpoken to on the fubject. He has heard of my being profecuted; but he little imagines it was for his crimes.

Thus, in the capital of America, amidft all its *vaunted liberty of the prefs*, and under the " *equal*" and " *humane*" laws of Pennfylvania, another man has been allowed to print and publifh, not only with impunity, but without reproof, a paragraph, for the re-publifhing of which, I have been feized as a criminal, expofed to the danger of a heavy fine, of imprifonment at hard labour, of being crammed in a dungeon, and *of suffering the punishment of a murderer*!

Is this your *republican* juftice! Is this the bleffed fruit of that *liberty*, to obtain which all the horrors of a revolution are to be encountered, kings are to be hurled from their thrones, and nations deluged in blood! Was it for this that America maintained a ten years defolating war;

war; that all the ties of interest, of allegiance, of friendship, and of nature were rent asunder, and that a hundred thousand of her sons were stretched dead on the plain!—Talk not to me of your sovereign people, and your universal sufferage; of your political liberty and your equal rights: they are empty sounds, which I regard not. Give me security for my person and property; or, at least, let me share the fate of my neighbour. " Send us (said the Israelites of old); " Send us, O Lord, a king, that he may render " us *justice*." To ensure this last mentioned inestimable blessing, is the end of civil society, and ought to be the great object of all political institutions. *Justice* is the soul of freedom, as *impartiality* is the soul of justice; and, without these, *liberty* is an impostor and *law* is a farce.

I should here bid the reader adieu, leaving him to pour out his soul, like Judge M'Kean, in hosannahs for the " temporal blessings of the " Representative Democracy, which the Al- " mighty, *in his great mercy*, has vouchsafed " unto us;" but I have pledged myself to prove, that *the British press is much free-er than that of America;* and, notwithstanding " the blessings, " in great mercy, vouchsafed unto us," I fear not, that, with the indulgence of the reader, I shall make good my promise. For the motives from which I do this I am responsible to no one: if, however, an apology is thought necessary, let it be sought for in the abominable treatment I have experienced.

Since the revolution, which terminated in the independence of these States, almost every publication

lication here, and every democratic one in Great Britain, has held the liberty of the American prefs up in triumphant exaltation over that of the prefs of Great Britain. How many volumes might be filled up with inflances of this fort! How many thoufand times is the vain boaft repeated in the courfe of each revolving fun! To refer to particular publications is like feeking for proofs of daylight or of darknefs : but, there is one that I muft refer to, hecaufe it fo aptly anfwers my purpofe. It is a letter of the arch fectarian PRIESTLEY, who, not content without companions in his fallen ftate, has fpared no pains to inveigle his countrymen hither. He tells the people of England, in this letter, fent there to be publifhed, that " *Here* (in *italicks* to mark the contraft) " *Here* the prefs is free. " *Here* truth is not a libel." This fatanic letter contains many other affertions equally *false*, which I may one day or other expofe ; but, at prefent, I notice only what appertains to my fubject.

The poor Doctor was always a bold afferter; but, in the cafe before us, I muft confefs, a more fcrupulous man might have been led into the adoption of a falfhood. The peal has been fo inceffantly rung in our ears. We have been fo bored with it in all feafons, at all hours, eating, drinking and fleeping time not excepted, that it required a degree of incredulity rarely to be met with to refift the temptation to belief. The affertion is, neverthelefs falfe ; and it is a falfhood too, which the fafety of every one (particularly *a foreigner*), who touches pen or types, requires to be clearly and fully expofed.

That

That TRUTH *may be a libel in Great Britain, and that it cannot be a libel here*, is generally believed; and is thought to conftitute the difference in the laws of the two countries, on this head. But this is no more than a vulgar notion, taken up from ignorance, and propagated from vanity and envy. I defy any man to produce me a fingle law, or a fingle conftitution (for, " thank God," as the Judge fays, we have many); I defy him to cite me a claufe or fentence, that fays, or that leaves room to fuppofe, that *truth* may not be deemed a libel, here as well as in England. The United States, and the individual States of Maffachufetts, New Hampfhire, Vermont, Maryland, North Carolina, and Kentuckey, each of them fay, that " the *press ought to* " *be free* " in a fhort vague fentence, of which any lawyer of a common capacity would give as many different interpretations as there can be rung changes upon twelve bells, which are faid to amount to fome millions. Pennfylvania and Tennefee fay the fame, and more. They fay, with the other States, and with the laws of England, that *the press shall be f ee ;* and they add, that " in profecutions for the publication of pa-
" pers, inveftigating the *official* conduct of *officers,*
" or where the matter publifhed is *proper for*
" *public i formation,* the *truth* thereof may be
" given in evidence." Connecticut, New York, New Jerfey, Delaware, Virginia, South Carolina, and Georgia, have had the prudence to fay nothing at all about the matter; and, as to Rhode Ifland, its conftitution is neither more nor lefs than a new edition of the Charter granted them by " the abundant grace, certain knowledge, and " mere motion" of King Charles II. Thus it
ftands,

ftands, bound up with the other fixteen conftitutions, without the addition or exclufion of a fingle word. And, all the other States, without one exception, have taken fpecial care to bind down their rulers *never to deprive them of the common law of England*, but to preferve it inviolate to them and their children. Amidft all their vagaries, when they were ftark ftaring drunk with revolutionary triumph, they had the good fenfe, the faving grace, to cling faft round this old trunk of folid and fubftantial liberty. Long may they hold by it, and never fuffer it to be chipped away by quibbling ftatutes and partial Judges!

Hence then, it happens, very luckily for me, that, if there be any State, in which the common law of England, refpecting libels, is departed from, it is poor Pennfylvania. And, what is the mighty " bleffing" fhe has had " vouchfafed " unto her?" Why, " in profecutions for the " publication of papers inveftigating the *official* " conduct of *officers*, or where the matter pub- " lifhed is *proper for public information*, the " *truth* may be *given in evidence.*" So that, you will pleafe to obferve, Meffieurs authors and printers, that, firft, the perfon about whom you publifh muft be *an officer ;* and next, you muft touch upon nothing but his *official* conduct. Precious privilege! It is a mere net to catch the unwary: it leaves not the leaft fcope for cenfuring any public man whatfoever, but feems, on the contrary, intended to fhelter his faults and his crimes from the lafh of the prefs. By declaring that the *truth* fhall be admitted as evidence as to fuch publications only as touch his *official* conduct, his private character and conduct are held up as facred and inviolable.

M But,

But, the Judge, the expositor of the constitution, goes still further. He tells us, that the publications, respecting the *official* conduct of officers, must not only be *true*, but " *candid*" and " *decent*" also. This is a maxim laid down in his charge, and every one will agree, that he was ready to put it in practice. Comfortable writing and publishing it must be, thus penned up with vague and indefinite epithets! *Truth* may be defined and ascertained, but what publication is there, which, by some quirk or other, might not be represented as *uncandid* or *indecent?*—Yet, as if this left the press still *too free*. The Judge tells us, that such publications, must not only be *decent, candid,* and *true*, but, besides all this, they must " have an eye *solely* to the *public good*.— Here is a pretty latitude for quibble and contestation! Not only the *facts* are to be established, and the *manner* and *stile* approved of by the court, but even the *motives* of the writer are to be enquired into, and may be construed into a ground for punishing him!

One would now think that the officers of Pennsylvania were safely enough fortified against the attacks of the press; but the Chief Justice was resolved to guard them at every point; and, therefore, after throwing up bastions in abundance and out-works upon out-works, he surrounds the whole with a line of contravalation, thus: " Where libels are printed against *persons employ-* " *ed in a public capacity*, they receive an *aggrava-* " *tion*, as they tend to *scandalize the government.*" Charming liberty of the press! Against men thus defended, what devil of a printer is there, who will ever dare to fire a single shot? Suppose, for
instance,

inftance, that a Judge were to be guilty of fome moft vile and infamous offence: fuppofe he were *to thieve;* one would think that a free prefs fhould take fome little notice of it; but you muft not do it, becaufe thieving is not (or, at leaft, I am fure, it ought not to be) the *official* conduct of a Judge, and therefore the truth cannot be given in evidence; and becaufe the libel would " receive an aggravation," as it would moft certainly " tend to *scandalize the government.*"— Thus is the prefs of Pennfylvania nailed down; but if fuch a thing had happened in England, or in France previous to the revolution, the printers would have blazoned it from one end of the empire, nay, from one end of the world to the other; and if they could have found a conveyance to the Moon, thither it would have went. It is right to curb fuch " licentious" fellows. Their blabbing ought to be prevented; and for doing this give me not a mighty kingdom with ftanding armies and letters de cachet, but give me a little fnug " Reprefentative Democracy," armed with the power of *binding them over at discretion,* and inflicting on them *the punishment of a murderer.*

As to the latter provifion of the claufe above quoted, that the *truths* publifhed muft be *proper for public information,* it is far worfe than nothing; for, what is *proper for public information* is no libel according to the common law, and therefore no *truth,* nor any evidence whatfoever, is neceffary to juftify its publication, in the eye of that law; but, according to the new maxim, what is very proper for public information may be a libel, if the truth of every word of it cannot be eftablifhed. I think

I think I have now satisfied the reader, that, in point of law, the American prefs has gained nothing over that of Great Britain. But, the Chief Juftice, as if he really intended to aid my undertaking, and to do away every doubt on the fubject, took good care to tell the Grand Jury, that, *with respect to libels, the common Law was confirmed and established by the Constitution itself.* Where then is the advantage derived from the new order of things ? If the conftitution of Pennfylvania, which is, according to the modern application of the word, the free-eft in America ; if this conftitution has done *no more* than confirm and eftablifh the common law of England, with refpect to the liberty of the prefs, how can any man have the impudence to boaft of that liberty being greater here than it is in England, where that fame common law ftill exifts in all its plenitude and purity, and is adminiftered by men the moft learned, independent and righteous in the world ?

Thus far then, the liberty of the prefs, is, in the eye *the law,* the fame in both countries ; but this does not prove, that there exift no circumftances in America, peculiar to it, which render the exercife of this liberty unfafe, and of courfe reftrains its operations. It is not only the principles profeffed in a country, that we are to look to, but alfo the *practice* of that country. The thing called the conftitution of France, for example, fays that the *free use* of the prefs is a right *sacred* and *inviolable* ; but this does not prevent the tyrants from feizing the printers by fcores, and tranfporting them without a trial and without a hearing.

The

The prefs has been, and ftill is, reftrained in this country, 1ft, by the notion, which has been, for evident motives, inculcated by artful men, that no *private character* ought to be publickly cenfured. 2nd, by the very dangerous privilege, which *foreign agents* poffefs, in having *a choice of governments*, under which to bring their profecutions. And, 3rd, by the terror, neceffarily excited in every printer, by the *disgraceful and cruel punishment*, to which he is liable.

As to the firft of thefe reftraints, nothing can give us a better idea of the extent to which it is carried, than the bold affertions contained in the Chief Judge's Charge. He tells us, that, though a publication may not reflect any moral turpitude on the party, it may yet be libellous, if it *thwarts the said party's desire of appearing agreeable in life*. This is a very comfortable doctrine to every *scoundrel*, and particularly to every *whore*, for you will not find one of either defcription, who does not defire *to appear agreeable in life*. The reafonablenefs of this doctrine his Honour fupports by telling us, that if any man does wrong, recourfe may be had to the courts of juftice, and that there can be no neceffity, *nor reason*, for appeals to the people in *news-papers* or *pamphlets*.

Thus, you fee, if his Honour fhuts up the prefs, he has the goodnefs to open his court to us. But, if I were to fee one officer of government go ftaggering drunk through the ftreet, on his return from a civic feftival; or another from the fame caufe, reeling into his feat, muft I hold my tongue, or go to law with them? If a fwindler, a man of the bafeft character, the moft treacherous and corrupt

rupt of mortals, were to propose himself as a candidate for a seat in the Legiflature, muft I say nothing about him; muft I not throw out even a hint to the people to warn them of their danger? If a Judge, or any other awful character, were to be detected in fhop-lifting, or in the commiffion of any fuch bafe and infamous crime; or if a lady were to choose, now and then, to relieve her hufband by retiring a few months to the arms of a friend, muft I few up my lips, and muft my prefs be as tame and contented as the cuckold himfelf?

Such may, indeed, be the practice of the American prefs; but is it that of the prefs of Great Britain. Only compare one of the London papers with an American paper, and you will foon fee which comes from the free-eft prefs. Is there a crime, is there a fault or a folly, which the editors and print-fellers in London do not lafh? They dive into every affembly and every houfe; they fpare characters neither public nor private; neither the people, the gentry, the clergy, the nobility nor the royal family itfelf, is fheltered from their ridicule or their cenfure. Let any American but open PETER PINDAR's works and the LONDON MORNING CHRONICLE; then let him read Judge M'Kean's Charge, and blufh at the boaft that has been fo often made about the liberty of the prefs.

I am far from approving of all, or of hardly any thing, contained in the works of Pindar and the Morning Chronicle: the Chronicle is the devoted tool of an infamous Jacobin faction, and the far greater part of Pindar's monotonous

odes

odes are an outrage on decency, on truth, and on every principle, moral and religious, by which a man of learning and talents ought to be directed. But, becaufe public cenfure and ridicule, when grounded on *falshood*, is unjuftifiable, it by no means follows, that the prefs is to exercife no fort of cenforfhip at all ; that it is not to record evil as well as righteous deeds ; that it is not to check the follies and vices of the times ; that it is not to exert its wholefome and mighty influence in fociety, but become the mere echo of the bench and the bar. No ; this does not follow; yet, this is the practice of the American prefs.

Come to my office, reader, and look over (if you have patience) the leaden fheets that are hither dragged from every quarter of the country. If they have one fingle fhaft of fatire, except it be on the old hackneyed fubject of kingcraft and prieft-craft, I will fuffer you to fuffocate me by reading me their contents.—And what is the reafon of this ? Is it that this bleffed " Reprefentative Democracy, which, *in great* " *mercy*, has been vouchfafed unto us," preferves us unfufceptible of folly or vice ? Is it that we are all wife, moral, religious, and pure as the driven fnow? Is it, my God ! that we know of no fuch thing as drunkennefs, adultery, fwindling, corruption, or blafphemy ? Or is it that we wifh to keep thefe things hidden from the world?—If this could be done, and if filence would produce a reformation, I would willingly confent,—not to become as tame and infipid as my brethren, but to throw my prefs into the river. But, this is impoffible ; fince whatever exifts, is,

and

and muſt be, known; and ſince wickedneſs the longer it remains unchaſtiſed, the more inveterate it becomes; ſince this is the caſe, the moſt rigid cenſorſhip in the preſs is abſolutely neceſſary, to check, in time, that which, if ſuffered to paſs unnoticed, will moſt certainly, ſooner or later, end in general degradation and ruin.

Yet, this timely check; this ſalutary and coſtleſs chaſtiſement, muſt remain a uſeleſs inſtrument in our hands, becauſe, forſooth, the villain and the ſtrumpet "*desire to appear agreeable in* "*life*," and becauſe an expoſure of their turpitude will "*ſtain the honour of their families*." For this cogent reaſon, the good and the bad, the upright ſtateſman and the traitor, the man of integrity and the rogue, the virtuous matron and the whore, are all to be jumbled to-gether, and the world is to take us in the lump, or nor at all.

But, may it pleaſe your Honour, this will not do. We know well, that the world is very ill-natured, and that, when it judges in the lump, it very ſeldom looks at the beſt ſide. Men of reputation, therefore, do not approve of this jumbling work. They wiſh to be diſtinguiſhed from thoſe that have none. This can be done only by the detecting of vice, and expoſing it to public cenſure; and I beg your Honour's leave to add one concluding obſervation of my own, which is this; *that I never yet knew a single person, man or woman, extremely anxious to restrain the liberty of the press, in this respect, who had not very sufficient reasons for so doing.*

The next reſtraint on the freedom of the American preſs, is, the very alarming privilege, which
foreign

foreign agents poſſeſs, in having *a choice of governments*, under which to bring their proſecutions.

I have already, in the former part of this pamphlet, ſaid how the preſs, in various parts of the country, has been kept in ſlavery by the unpuniſhed violences of the domineering French faction; and, in the relation of the treatment I have met with, I have clearly proved what every printer, of any independence of ſpirit has to expect from another quarter. This ſituation of things, however, has been produced by a combination of ſingular circumſtances, and it may probably wear away as thoſe circumſtances change. But, the evil, of which I have now to complain, is of a nature not to be worn away by the hand of time alone. It is built on law and conſtitution, or, at leaſt, it operates as if it were, and admits of no remedy, except by ſome poſitive act of a convention or the legiſlature.

It was hoped (though, it muſt be confeſſed, with very little reaſon), that America, when ſeparated from Great Britain, would never more be affected by the quarrels of European nations. PAINE told the people, that they would have nothing to do but grow rich, while other nations ſhould be at war. " Our commerce," ſays he, " will always ſecure us the *peace and friendſhip* of " all Europe." This, by woeful experience, we find to have been like all the reſt of ſhallowheaded Paine's predictions. But, this is not the worſt. Not only does America feel the preſſure of European wars, in a degree equal to that felt by the people of Great Britain at this moment;

but she is curfed with a foreign faction in her bosom, by which she is continually curbed, harrassed, injured, insulted, and betrayed.

The politics of the country are become so connected, so interwoven, with the politics of other nations, France in particular, that they are never spoken of in any other than a relative light. I verily believe, and indeed I am certain, that, as to numbers, men are more equally divided, at this time, between the Federal government and the French, than they were in the year 1778, between the Congress and the King of England.

Nor does this pernicious division stop here. The State governments have their sides. One State is called a *Federal State* and another an *Antifederal State*; and it is notorious, that the politics of the persons, who administer these subaltern governments, are generally fixed and uniform on one side or the other.

In such a state of things, only think of the danger of allowing foreign ministers and agents *to choose the government, under which to bring their prosecutions!* Possessing this dreadful privilege, will not every foreign agent take good care to institute his prosecutions under that government, to which the party prosecuted has, by his politics, rendered himself obnoxious? And, where this can be done, what sort of chance, I pray, is there for a man who meddles with the press, and who happens to be situated in a State, where he must of necessity be obnoxious to one of the two governments, under which he lives?

My

My own cafe is a ftriking exemplification of
the danger of this privilege. Yrujo the Spaniard
applied firft to the Federal Government to profecute me, and was informed that it would be
done in the Federal courts. But, this he remon-
ftrated againft, and requefted that it might be
done in the courts of Pennfylvania; in which
courts M'Kean is Chief Judge.—Now, why this
requeft? Why prefer one jurifdiction to another?
The courts are held at the fame place, and nearly at the fame time. The Judges of the Federal
court are men famous for their learning and their
integrity; and, I am fure, ordering the trial in
this court ought to have been looked upon as a
mark of refpect to the Spanifh King. How,
then, are we to account for this extraordinary
requeft?

Leaving the reader to account for it in his
own way, I fhall tell him that the requeft was
refufed; and that, then, a new profecution was
fet on foot under the government of Pennfylvania. The matter contained in the above bill of
Indictment was hunted out; and, let it be well
remembered, that every pretended libel contained in this bill, was publifhed *before I was
bound over on the firft complaint.* In poffeffion
of this fact, the reader will be able to guefs what
the hopes of the profecutor were founded on.

The matter in the bill of indictment, if libellous, was furely fo before I was bound over the
firft time. How comes it then, that it was not
included in the firft complaint? This puzzled
the Grand Jury. The thing appeared fo unna-
tural to them, that they fent for the two Attorneys
General

General to explain the myſtery; when it was found, that they had taken care, in drawing their indictments, to ſteer clear of each other; in doing which I, by-the-bye, do not mean to hint, that either of theſe gentlemen did any more than his duty.

Thus was ſeen the ſingular phenomenon of a printer proſecuted by *two governments*, at one and the ſame time, for different parts of one and the ſame offence! And this is *American liberty of the preſs!*

Did Engliſhmen ever hear of any thing of this kind before? No; they have *one* Government, *one* law, and *one* conſtitution, for all. In their country, neither foreigner nor native, plaintiff nor defendant, has a choice of juriſdictions, tribunals, or judges. Where the offence is committed, there muſt it be tried. They have no claſhing of governments of oppoſite politics, under which every printer is in hourly danger, from the intrigues of foreign agents, and is obliged to tack and ſhift, like a polacre with contending winds between Sylla and Charibdis. No; in England, all is fair and free. The path is ſimple: the law is one and the ſame, and is equal in its operations in every place and towards all parties. It is founded in wiſdom and in juſtice, and is adminiſtered with candour, impartiality, and mercy.

The third reſtraint on the liberty of the American preſs, and the laſt which I ſhall notice, *at this time*, is, *the fear which muſt be naturally excited in every writer and printer, by the disgraceful and cruel puniſhment, to which he is continually exposed.* After

After all that we have heard and feen about the *mildness* and *humanity* of the American laws; after all the cant of the *tender-hearted* Briffot; after all the filly eulogiums on the prifons of Philadelphia, fpread abroad in pamphlets, fpeeches, and paragraphs; and after all the farcaftic and acrimonious invective which the American prefs is continually pouring out againft the *sanguinary* code of Great Britain: bored with all this, I fay, even to furfeiting, my prefent complaint muft appear very extraordinary. Let it. All that I have to do, is to prove it well founded.

The liberty of doing any thing, is greater or lefs, in proportion to the punifhment that the law awards for it. I am, therefore, far from pretending that the Americans do not, in fome refpects, poffefs more liberty than the Englifh. They are in lefs danger, when they fteal, rob, forge, coin, and murder; for, thefe crimes are here punifhed with *fine, jail imprisonment, imprisonment at hard labour*, or *solitary confinement;* whereas, in England, they are punifhed with *death*. But, let thofe, who have reafon, boaft of this fort of liberty. It is not what I want. I only contend for liberty to write and to print.

This liberty is a right, fanctioned by law, as far as a certain line, all beyond which is called libelling. This line reaches, as I have clearly proved, juft as far in America as it does in England, and no farther. All that we have to do then is to fee, which country inflicts punifhments the *least severe* on tranfgreffors; for, in that country the prefs muft be *most free*.

By

By only casting our eyes on the Chief Judge's Charge, we shall perceive, that the punishments are ten fold more severe in America than in England. In England, a transgressor of the laws of the press, or, in other words, a libeller, is punishable by *fine*, by *imprisonment in jail*, by *standing in the pillory;* or by any two, or all three, of them. But, what is his punishment in America? Why, in the first place, *fine* and *jail imprisonment,* as in England, and to these may be added, imprisonment *at hard labour*, and even *solitary confinement in a dungeon*, at the *discretion of the court;* and all this too in a country, where the prosecutor may have *a choice of courts* !

As far as relates to *fines* and *jail imprisonment,* the code of the two countries is the same; but, instead of the momentary shame of the pillory, the American libeller, whether writer or printer, is liable to the lasting pain and disgrace of hard labour, and to the more horrid punishment of the dungeon. Standing in the pillory, which is the worst an English libeller can undergo, is over in a few hours. The sufferer is then placed in jail, where he is as free as a detention of his person will admit of. He can see, hear, read and converse. He is at ease; can be visited by his friends; nay, *Callender* (the run-away Scotchman) boasts, that his associates even fold their libels in Newgate. What is this punishment compared to continual *hard labour* ? And what is hard labour, or any thing else, compared to being thrown into a cell, and cut off, not only from friends and family, but from every human being?

But,

But, we muft not drop the fubject here. Punifhments, as to their influence in fociety, and confequently as to their reftraint on the prefs, muft be confidered *relatively*; for, what may be a very light punifhment in one country, may be a very heavy, and even a very cruel one, in another. In England, for inftance, robbery, forgery, murder, &c. are punifhed with *death:* in America thefe crimes are punifhed with *hard labour,* or *solitary confinement.* So that, to inflict thefe latter punifhments on a libeller *here,* is exactly as cruel as it would be to inflict death on him in England.

What were the motives of the rulers, who leffened the punifhment for *murder,* and other horrid crimes, while they augmented the punifhment for *libelling,* I muft leave thofe to determine, who boaft fo much about the liberty of their prefs; but, this I will undertake to fay, that it is moft excellently well calculated to reftrain, intimidate, and over awe, every one who has any thing to do with writing and printing. What man will ever dare to communicate his thoughts to the public, while it is probable, or even *poffible,* that his writing will procure him a place in that " *temple* of *humanity*," as it has been called, the Philadelphia prifon; where, dreffed in a jail uniform, penned up amongft run-away thieving negro flaves; amongft robbers, forgers, fodomites, and murderers; where, in fhort, amongft convicts of every colour and of every crime, he is employed in the polite art of pounding hemp, with the infinite fatisfaction of being exhibited to travelling *philanthropists* as a " living monu-
" ment of American *mildness* and *humanity*"?—
And

And, if this be too much for a man of reputation and talents to bear, how fhall he dare to brave the horrors of a cell; to be fecluded from friends, parents, wife, children, and all that renders life worth poffeffing ; to be barred up for months, or for years, like a condemned malefactor ; and this too at the difcretion of a court, chofen, perhaps, by his profecutor?

Did Englifhmen . . . . but, why do I purfue in the odious comparifon?—Did even Frenchmen ever feel a reftraint like this?—The Baftile!—It was bad enough, to be fure ; but, a writer confined there, had, at leaft, the confolation of knowing, that he was diftinguifhed from felons and murderers. Though far too feverely punifhed, he was not covered with everlafting difgrace and infamy. Literature, though the abufe of it was cruelly chaftifed, was not degraded, was not rendered at once hateful and defpicable, as it is by the indifcriminating code of Pennfylvania.

Yet, notwithftanding all we have feen, the Chief Judge has the modefty to tell the Grand Jury, from the bench, that " the criminal law of " *this State* is fo pregnant with *juftice*, fo agree- " able to *reafon*, fo full of *equity* and *clemency*, " that even thofe who fuffer by it, *cannot charge* " *it with rigour*"!!!—This was too much. He might, at any rate, have fpared us the mortification of liftening to this. But, it is the fafhion. Almoft every public harrangue has fome fuch vaunting conclufion. It may be good policy, to be fure, as it tends, to keep the people here in excellent humour, while it excites envy in thofe

of

of ther nations, makes them difcontented whit
their lot, and invites them to cultivate the deferts
of America; but then, the greateft care imagin-
able fhould be taken, not to lay the iron finger
on fuch men as are not formed for paffive fuf-
france, and particularly if they are Britons; for
they, above all others, will not whifper their
curfes to the winds: they will turn their eyes
towards their native land: they will compare
what they have loft with what they have gained;
nor will all the terrors of hard labour and a Philadelphia dungeon, ever, I truft, deter them from
proclaiming the account to the world.

I have now accomplifhed my object. I have
expofed the conduct of my enemies, and I have
amply proved, that the prefs is more free in
Great Britain than it is in America. As to the
motives by which I have been actuated, though
I frankly confefs, that had I not been injured,
had I not been fingled out as an object of legal
vengeance, no part of this pamphlet would ever
have been written or thought of; yet, I am far
from wifhing to throw an odium on the people
of thefe States in general, and to reprefent them
as a tame degenerate race of mortals. On the
contrary, I know that a very great majority of
them have felt, and expreffed, the utmoft indignation at the treatment I have received. The
decifion of the Grand Jury alone, confidering
the charge that was made to them, is fufficient
to prove, that the fpirit of true liberty is yet alive
on this fide the Atlantic. That decifion, and the
joy which it excited amongft all the refpectable
inhabitants of the city of Philadelphia, are frefh
in every one's memory, and will, I am fure, be

for

for ever rivetted in mine. Let it not be suppoſed, however, that I ſay this with the baſe motive of procuring or preſerving *patronage,* either public or private. I ſtand in need of none. My good honeſt parents taught me the labours of the field, and, with theſe, they taught me independence of mind. It has pleaſed God to bleſs me with health, and with limbs to gain my bread; and, while I am able to do this by the ſpade or the plough, I will never ſeek for wealth nor for eaſe, by fawning for popular favour, or by burying my injuries in ſilent ſubmiſſion.